HENRY PURCELL

I. HENRY PURCELL
(From an oil-painting attributed to Sir Godfrey Kneller)

By kind permission of the late W. Barclay Squire.

HENRY PURCELL

By

DENNIS ARUNDELL

M.A., Mus.B.
Fellow of St. John's College, Cambridge

GREENWOOD PRESS, PUBLISHERS
WESTPORT, CONNECTICUT

Originally published in 1927
by Oxford University Press, London

First Greenwood Reprinting 1971

Library of Congress Catalogue Card Number 72-114454

SBN 8371-4752-2

Printed in the United States of America

TO THE MEMORY OF

W. BARCLAY SQUIRE

WITHOUT WHOSE HELP AND KINDNESS

THIS BOOK COULD NEVER HAVE

BEEN WRITTEN

CONTENTS

LIST OF ILLUSTRATIONS

Rebus on Mr. *Henry Purcell's* Name, by Mr. *Tomlinson*

Sett to Musick by Mr. *John Lenton.*

The Mate to a Cock, and Corn tall as Wheat
is his Christian Name, who in Musick's Compleat ;
his Sirname begings (*sic*) with the Grace of a Cat,
and concludes with the House of a Hermit note that ;
his Skill and Performance each Auditor Wins,
but the Poet deserves a good kick on the Shins.

Galli marita par tritico seges,
Praenomen est ejus, dat chromati leges
Intrat cognomen,—blanditiis Cati,
Exit Eremi in Aedibus stali (*sic*),
Expertum effectum omnes admirentur
Quid merent Poetae ? ut bene calcentur.

Pleasant Musical Companion.

To his unknown Friend, Mr. Henry Purcell.

. . . Thus I unknown my Gratitude express,
And conscious Gratitude could pay no less.
This Tribute from each *British Muse* is due,
Our whole Poetic Tribe's oblig'd to you.
For where the Author's scanty Words have fail'd,
Your happier Graces, *Purcell,* have prevail'd.
And surely none but you with equal Ease
Could add to *David,* and make *Durfy* please.

T. Brown.
Playford's *Harmonia Sacra.*

Purcell and his Family

ACCORDING to tradition the first Norman to land at Pevensey and the first to win guerdon land from the Conqueror was a Purcell. But the name does not occur in the Battle Abbey Roll, and there is apparently no record of his having been made hereditary usher of the King's chamber or of his founding the baronial family, which is said to have lasted over a hundred years.[1] From this legendary invader sprang several families in Ireland and England, and from the Purcells of Shropshire, according to Hart, who apparently has no proof to produce, came the family which settled in London and into which Henry Purcell was born. Despite various attempts to solve the mystery of his ancestry none of the fantastic tales or hopeful theories has produced any definite facts, and the earliest detail that can be proved to belong to Henry Purcell's family is that Edward, his brother, was born in 1653.[2] There is no mention of a Purcell among the Singing Men of the Abbey who took the Covenant in 1645, and Henry Purcell the elder is first recorded as having acted in D'Avenant's experimental opera

---

[1] *Irish Landed Gentry when Cromwell came to Ireland*, 2nd ed., Dublin, 1887. Those who are interested will find innumerable Purcell pedigrees in vol. vii of the Association for the Preservation of the Memorials of the Dead, and Hart's *Irish Pedigrees*—where Charlemagne is cited as an ancestor.

[2] The 'Mr. Purcell' who was a ratepayer in Westminster in 1641, 1651, 1656, and 1659 was presumably Henry Purcell the elder. But so much muddle has been already made by guesses as to the life and family of Henry Purcell that it is unsafe to take this for granted, especially as the *Administration Act Books* record a William Parsell (the spelling always varies) as the brother of Thomas Parsell of the Precincts of the Tower of London, who died in 1635. This William died in 1645, but what of his family? Was he a relation of Henry the elder?

The Siege of Rhodes in 1656. Towards the end of the year 1659 his second son, Henry, was born.[1]

On 21 Feb. 1660 Pepys

' met with Mr. Lock and Pursell, Masters of Music, and with them to the Coffee House, into a room next the water, by ourselves, where we spent an hour or two. . . . Here we had variety of brave Italian and Spanish songs, and a canon for eight voices, which Mr. Lock had lately made on these words : " Domine salvum fac Regem ", an admirable thing.'

Purcell became a Gentleman of the Chapel Royal at the re-establishment of that musical training-ground [2] and was made a Composer for the Violins and Master of the Abbey Choristers, while his brother Thomas, also a Gentleman of the Chapel Royal, who as such sang with his brother at the coronation of Charles II, was appointed a member of the King's Private Musick and also held the posts of lay vicar and copyist at Westminster Abbey. The only facts that have been gleaned of the next two years, apart from the birth of a daughter Katherine [3] to Henry Purcell, are records dealing with the fees paid and due to the two brothers for their livery as Musicians in Ordinary and members of the Private Musick.

Henry Purcell the elder died on 11 Aug. 1664 in his house in ' Great Almery South ',[4] where the Gentlemen of the Choir had their residence. For the next five years the only Purcell records that remain deal with the payments that were and were

[1] The inscription on Henry Purcell's tomb, ' anno aetatis suae 37mo ', proves him to have been born between 21 Nov. 1658 and 20 Nov. 1659 for him to be in his thirty-seventh year on 21 Nov. 1695, and the fact that the *Sonatas* were published in June 1683, ' aet. suae 24 ', narrows the time still further to between June and 20 Nov. 1659.

[2] De la Fontaine, *The King's Musick, passim.*

[3] Bap. 13 March 1662.

[4] Rate-Books of St. Margaret's, Westminster, *et passim.*

not made to Thomas Purcell as one of the ' Musitians that doe service in the Chappell Royall, whose Salleryes are paid in the Treasury of His Majesty's Chamber '.[1] The poor musicians were not exempt from the specious hopes held out by Charles to all his servants and ministers, though, when petitioned by Thomas Purcell in 1666 for some money with which to pay the Chapel Royal staff, the king writes that he ' thinks his honour concerned therein, and therefore wishes full and punctual payment of all that is due to them, on the next assignment of moneys to the Treasurer of the Chamber '.[2] The accounts that deal with the King's Musick do, it is true, include several records of payments, but, though for example these occur under Thomas Purcell's name from 1662 to 1667, the same sums are still owing ten years later. At times the bad debts could be shouldered on to others—as when Thomas Purcell with two other musicians of the Private Musick petitioned that the arrears due to them from His Majesty's Great Wardrobe for the years 1669, 1670, and 1671, might be assigned to their fellow musician, Humphrey Madge, to whom, no doubt, they were in debt.[3] He would at least be no worse off by the transaction and would moreover have the dubious satisfaction of being a creditor of royalty.

Young Henry Purcell comes into view for a moment in 1670. He is said to have set to music the *Address of the Children of the Chapel Royal to the King and Captain Cook on his Majesty's birthday*. He was, after his father's death, brought up by his uncle, perhaps still living with his mother in her house in ' Tuttle St.'—where she moved after her husband's death—and was getting his first musical education from the intolerably conceited Captain Cook, who was Master of the Children till his death in 1672.

---

[1] *King's Musick,* 209. [2] Cal. State Papers, Dom.
[3] *King's Musick,* 235.

The next two years show Thomas Purcell well established in the world of court music. With Pelham Humphrey he was in charge of the King's band of violins, and the word of these two ' Composers in Ordinary ' was upheld by a royal order :

' Whereas his Majesty is displeased that the violins neglect their duty in attending in his Chappell Royall, it is ordered that if any of the violins shall neglect to attend, either to practice or to wayte in the Chappell, whensoever they have received notice from Mr. Purcell or Mr. Humphryes, that for such fault they shall be suspended their places.' (2 July 1672.) [1]

Henry Purcell's voice broke in 1673 and he therefore had to leave the Chapel Royal. But he was at once appointed

' keeper, maker, mender, repayrer and tuner of the regalls, organs, virginalls, flutes and recorders and all other kind of wind instruments whatsoever, in ordinary, without fee, to his Majesty, and assistant to John Hingston, and upon the death or other avoydance of the latter, to come in ordinary with fee '.[2]

As a ' late child of his Majesty's Chappell Royall, whose voice is changed, and gon [*sic*] from the Chappell ' [3] he was to be paid £30 a year and was at once provided with fine holland, hand-kerchiefs, a felt hat and, four years later, ' one and twenty ells, three quarters of holland, for four whole shirts, four half shirts and four bands and cuffs '.

Henry's elder brother, Edward, now appears in the character of ' Gentleman Usher Daily Waiter Assistant ' [4] and apparently had the job of ' making ready of standing houses and progress houses in the (King's) remove '. Thomas seems to have had the knack of collecting posts vacated by the deaths of various musicians : for in 1674 payments were made to ' Thomas Purcell in the place of Henry Lawes . . . Thomas Purcell in the

[1] *King's Musick*, 245. [2] Ibid. 255.
[3] Ibid. 263. [4] Treasury Books, *et passim*.

place of Dr. John Wilson . . . Thomas Purcell in the place of George Hudson'.[1] He was also Groom of the Robes, a 'tenner' in the Chapel Royal, he superintended the music for Charles II at Windsor and was responsible for engaging the famous organ-builder, Bernhardt Schmidt, otherwise known as Father Smith, put up an organ in the private chapel at Windsor.

At the age of seventeen Henry Purcell was given the very responsible post of copyist at the Abbey. In these days of innumerable music publishers it can be realized how difficult it must have been at the time of the Restoration for music to progress, and how enthusiastic and persevering musicians had to be if they were to learn anything about music of their own day or of earlier times. Publishing was then a very expensive business—as Purcell found to his cost in later years [2]—and musicians had inevitably to transcribe the works they wished to play or study. Did this lead to better musicianship? Was Purcell the greater writer because of his early conscious or unconscious steeping in the great number of compositions he must have copied? He was young enough not to realize the responsibility of his task and the responsibility was even greater than appears at first sight.

In the Civil War the parliamentary troops had indulged their obedient or fanatical terrorism in making a dead set at anything in the churches and cathedrals that seemed to point to idolatry. Images and ornamentation naturally roused them to fury, and in their enthusiasm they destroyed thousands of music-books, so that the long tradition of choristers and singing-men was broken. The loss of the books of anthems not only meant a sudden increase in the value of the copies that remained, but it also entailed more work for the copyists of the large churches and cathedrals. Purcell would in the ordinary course of his job as copyist have had to copy out the parts for

[1] *King's Musick*, 279.   [2] See p. 71.

the choir, and occasionally transcribe a new anthem, but, as things were, he would have to write out many anthems which had to be borrowed from whatever church or person had been lucky enough to keep a copy—perhaps now a unique copy— of a popular or exceptional work. The arduous task must have been invaluable for him, whether he realized it or not at the time,[1] and his connexion with the Abbey would inevitably bring him in touch with Dr. Blow, the organist—if he had not already come under him at the Chapel Royal. Dr. Burney imagined that Purcell was made organist at Westminster at this time, but he must have made the slip by thinking that his connexion with the Abbey implied his playing the organ— though it is true that Dr. Blow was made organist of the Chapel Royal in this year and it is conceivable that Purcell occasionally deputized for him at the Abbey.

In the August of 1677 Matthew Lock—the great experimenter in English Opera and enthusiastic supporter of sensible innovations [2]—died, and his post as Composer in Ordinary for the Violin was given in the following month to young Henry Purcell.[3] The first recorded work of Henry Purcell's— not counting the song *Sweet Tyraness*, which was published in Playford's *Musical Companion* when he was only eight years old, and which was therefore fairly certainly written by his father— was his eleven-year-old production, the *Address of the Children*, and his first published work was a song in Playford's *Choice Ayres, Songs and Dialogues*, Book I, 1676. But the first composition of any size was written at the time of his appointment as Composer in Ordinary—an *Elegy* on the death of his famous predecessor, which was published two years later in the

---

[1] See p. 135.

[2] See *Cupid and Death, Psyche*, his very bitter *Modern Church Music* and *The Present Practice of Music Vindicated*.

[3] *King's Musick*, 322.

second Book of the *Choice Ayres.* In all probability when this work was sung his younger brother, Daniel, took part, for he was at the time a child of the Chapel Royal : his voice had probably not broken by 1678,[1] as his name is included in a list of the children of the Chapel who attended the King at Windsor from 14 Aug. to 26 Sept. in that year, for which he was paid £6 12s.[2]

Thomas Purcell in these years only emerges through the records of payments made to the musicians, but on 13 Dec. 1679 there is an entry which is of more interest than the usual payment of £16 2s. 6d. for livery. From a list made on this date of the musicians who were paid by the treasurer of the great wardrobe—giving the amounts of their wages per annum—Thomas Purcell is shown as earning £46 10s. 10d. as a member of the violins, £42 15s. as Composer of the Violins, £46 10s. 10d. as a member of the Private Musick, and £36 2s. 6d.—again as a member of the Private Musick.[3] If this list is authoritative his whole salary as a musician can be reckoned at £171 19s. 2d. per annum. In addition he was paid a regular livery fee of £16 2s. 6d.—drawing, as we have seen, livery fees for other members of the music who were dead—and as Groom of the Robes he received £60. His total salary must have been about £250—quite an adequate income in those days ; but, as the records show, he probably never was paid anything approaching that sum—and what he did get was usually in arrears.

The year 1680 marks a great change in the affairs of Henry Purcell. It is true that his private life does not come into view in any detail—his whole history and the history of his ancestors and descendants seem inevitably and maliciously hidden, and we have to be as content as we can with occasional

---

[1] If Daniel's voice was not broken by 1678 the traditional year of his birth, 1660, must be wrong : it should be re-dated at least two years later.

[2] *King's Musick*, 339.   [3] Ibid. 345.

records of births, deaths, and payments. But in this year he suddenly appears as a composer, and until his death fifteen years later there is no falling-off in quantity or quality of his musical works.

In this year he wrote his first music for the theatre. The occasion was the production of the heroic play *Theodosius*. The first performance was well received and so played on the feelings of the ladies of the audience with its innocent heroine—played by the incomparable Mrs. Barry—who takes poison in her wedding dress, that it became well known as a favourite with the fair sex and, in a list of books compiled by the *Spectator* (No. 92, Friday, 15 June) for ladies to read, *Theodosius* actually ' carries it from all the rest '. Purcell's contribution to this successful piece consists chiefly of a big introductory ritual scene

—' *A stately Temple, which represents the Christian Religion as in its first Magnificence. . . . The Side Scenes shew the horrid Tortures with which the* Roman *Tyrants persecuted the Church; and the flat Scene, which is the Limit of the Prospect, discovers an Altar richly adorn'd, before it* Constantine, *suppos'd kneels with Commanders about him, gazing at a bloody Cross in the Air. . . . Instruments are heard and many Attendants : the Ministers at Divine Service walk busily up and down till* Atticus *the Chief of all the Priests, and Successor of St.* Chrysostom, *in rich Robes, comes forward with the Philosopher* Leontine; *the Waiters in Ranks bowing all the way before them.*'

I have quoted this description at some length to show a typical example of the craze for pictorial spectacle that held sway in the theatre of the day. But, though this is typical, the Tortures, bloody Cross, and Waiters are as nothing compared with the glories that are found in the later plays to which Purcell wrote music, as will soon be seen in the discussion on his Dramatic Music. It is essential to realize this attitude of Restoration audiences towards plays, for it is absolutely typical of the superficial nature of the day. The wonder is that Purcell managed to write good music and that it was recognized at the time as good music, for it was the tendency in the theatre, the church, and private house to live on the fringe of things. Elizabethan enthusiasm had died out, and society manners were coming into fashion. Music was in a sense popular. Songs, dances, and masques were dragged unmercifully into plays that perhaps were quite unfitted for them, and, as long as the eye and ear were tickled, nobody cared whether Dryden made Shakespeare actable or whether D'Urfey was coarse. It was becoming fashionable for leaders of society to give musical at-homes—music meetings they were called ; but, though the most eminent composer that was available might be used as an additional attraction, the chief interests were small talk, secret assignations with some one else's wife, and ignorantly fulsome praise of the host's latest song. In *The Wives' Excuse*, to which Purcell wrote music in 1691, there is an admirable scene at a Music Meeting.

Friendall. Ladies and gentlemen, how do you like the music ?
Mrs. Sightly. O very fine sure, sir.
Mrs. Witwoud. What say you to 't, young gentleman ?
Springame. I have something to say to you, I like a great
     deal better, provided you won't laugh at me. [*Going
     aside with her.*] But the music's extremely fine. [*To the
     company.*]
Wellvile. Especially the vocal part. For I did not under-
     stand a word on't.
Friendall. Nor I, faith, *Wellvile*, but the words were *Italian*,
     they sung well, and that 's enough for the pleasure of the
     ear. . . . *Wilding*, thou hast been so busy about that young
     girl there, thou know'st nothing of the matter.
Wilding. O, sir, you're mistaken, I am a great admirer—
Friendall. Of every thing in petticoats.
Wilding. Of these musical entertainments ; I am very
     musical, and love any call that brings the women together.

Wilding is, as it happens, exceptionally honest, for he immediately confesses that he thought sonatas and chaconnes might
be two Italian fiddlers of Mr. Friendall's acquaintance.

I have made this digression to insist on the atmosphere in
which Purcell wrote his music. Judging by the quantity alone
of his compositions it would seem that he found a musician's
life very easy—as no doubt he did in those days which were
ruled, superficially at any rate, by any tickling fancy—and the
quality of his work would seem to imply that his audiences
' knew a good thing when they saw it ', but the inconsiderate
attitude and thistledown mentality displayed by the majority
of the audiences make it all the more wonderful that the
Restoration produced any composer of standing.

The year 1680 was altogether a notable one in Purcell's life.
Apart from his first dramatic composition, it saw the production of his first Court Odes or Welcome Songs and his appointment as organist of Westminster Abbey. His appointment as
organist is said to have come about from the resignation of
Dr. Blow in favour of his brilliant pupil. If this is so—and
there is no reason to suppose the tale to be false—Dr. Blow
must have been a remarkably far-seeing musician and an un-
usually great man to resign a good post in the prime of his life
to the twenty-year-old Purcell who was twelve years his junior.

At about this time Purcell, who was now living in Great
St. Ann's Lane,[1] married.[2] His wife was in all probability

---

[1] In 1681 he had his house assessed at 8s. after the general assessment
had been made ; in 1682 he was paying 16s. rent for a house in Great St.
Ann's Lane (St. Ann's Street in modern times), so presumably he moved
to this house towards the end of 1681. From December 1681 to December
1683 he was paid by the Dean and Chapter £2 a quarter (the usual sum)
' in lieu of a house ' in Dean's Yard.

[2] His son, John Baptista, was baptized on 9 Aug. 1682. The power of
attorney granted to Matthew, son of Thomas Purcell, on 15 May 1681, was

a Frances Peters,[1] whose family had been connected with the parish of St. Margaret's, Westminster, for over a hundred years. The year 1681 saw the production of his second Welcome Song for the King, and the following year, after attending His Majesty at Windsor with the King's Musick, he was appointed organist of the Chapel Royal. His uncle, Thomas, died at the end of July, and about two months later Henry Purcell's son, John Baptista, born a week after Thomas Purcell was buried, died and was buried in the cloisters of Westminster Abbey. But four days later Charles came back to town from his usual summer visit to Newmarket and Purcell had to produce yet another Welcome Song.

In 1683 Purcell was made one of the King's Composers and in his new capacity published his *Sonnatas in III Parts* for two violins and bass. The Rye House Plot was the inspiration for his Welcome Song *Fly, Bold Rebellion*; the marriage of Prince George of Denmark and the future Queen Anne was celebrated by Purcell with an Ode *From hardy climes and dangerous toils of war*; and for St. Cecilia's Day, 22 Nov., of this year, Purcell wrote three works, *Welcome to all the Pleasures, Raise, raise the Voice*, and *Laudate Ceciliam*.

At the end of the year he was appointed, according to the warrant dated 16 Feb. 1684,—

witnessed by ' F. Purcell ', but unfortunately this cannot date the marriage more definitely, as there was a Francis Purcell who was admitted as a Groom in Ordinary on 11 Feb. 1680 (Calendar of State Papers). He may have been the witness, and possibly was a relative.

[1] Their daughter, Mary Peters, was presumably named after her mother's family, and a monument to a Robert Peter (*c*. 1553) in the church of St. Margaret shows the same arms as those on Frances Purcell's tomb : Gules, on a bend or between two escallops argent, a Cornish Chough enclosed by as many cinquefoils argent—except that on Frances Purcell's tomb the escallops are omitted.

' keeper, maker, repairer and mender and tuner of all and every his Majesty's musicall wind instruments ; that is to say all regalls, virginalls, organs, flutes, recorders and all other kind of wind instruments whatsoever, in the place of John Hingston, deceased.'

His wages were to be £60 a year apart from all his expenses connected with the ' workinge, labouringe, makeing and mending any of the instruments aforesaid '. He was further authorized

' to take up within ye realme of England all such metalls, wyer, waynscote and other wood and things as shalbe [*sic*] necessary to be imployed about the premisses, agreeing, paying and allowing reasonable rates and prices for the same. And also in his Majesty's name and upon reasonable and lawfull prices, wages and hire, to take up such workmen, artificers, labourers, worke and store houses, land and water carriages and all other needefull things as the said Henry Purcell or his assignes shall thinke convenient to be used on ye premisses. And also power and authority to the said Henry Purcell or his assignes to take up all tymber, strings, and feathers, necessary and convenient for the premisses, agreeing, paying and allowing reasonable rates and prices for the same, in as full and ample manner as the said John Hingston . . . formerly had.' [1]

On paper this warrant gave Purcell considerable power, and no doubt the office was fairly important as it certainly was responsible ; but it must have been hard to work and to get others to work under promise of royal payment. Possibly the man who held many offices was in a better position to expect a certain percentage of his fees than a one-job man. Purcell, like his uncle, collected post after post. He was now Organist of Westminster Abbey, Organist and Singer at the Chapel Royal, Copyist at the Abbey for the second time,

[1] *King's Musick*, 364–5 ; *L. C.*, vol. 749, p. 23.

a King's Composer, and member of the King's Musick, Keeper and Mender of the instruments, and he now shared with Blow the honour of introducing the new organ at the Temple. This instrument had been built by Bernhardt Schmidt, who had already made the organ for Windsor, in competition with the rival builder Renatus Harris. Schmidt's instrument was preferred, not only because the two players he got to perform on it were even better than the famous John Baptist Draghi who played on the rival instrument, but because, in addition to its compass, it had two additional quarter-tones in each octave that made it possible for remote keys to be used [1] ' which rarityes no other organ in England hath ; and can play any tune, as, for instance, ye tune of ye 119th Psalm (in E minor), and severall other services set by excellent musicians ; which no other organ will do '.[2]

On 23 April 1685 James II was crowned. For this occasion Purcell wrote the anthem *My heart is inditing*, which was performed with an earlier work *I was glad when they said unto me*, and superintended the erection of the organ for the coronation. He was paid £34 12s. out of the secret service money—which was used for all extraordinary royal occasions—

' for so much money by him disbursed and craved for providing and setting up an organ in the abbey church of

[1] It must be remembered that at this time—indeed, up to the middle of the nineteenth century—most keyboard instruments were tuned according to the Meantone temperament. This system gave approximate accuracy only to the following notes :

Schmidt added the notes A♭ and D♯, and so increased the list of tolerable keys by four—two major and two minor.

[2] Lahee, *The Organ and its Masters.*

Westm[r]. for the solemnity of the coronation, and for the removing the same, and other services performed in his said Ma'ties chappell since the 25th of March, 1685, according to a bill signed by the Bishop of London.' [1]

In August he was sworn in as ' harpsicall-player ' in the private music of the new king,[2] and for James's birthday, 14 Oct., he prepared a congratulatory ode—a precedent which he followed till his death—which was performed at Whitehall among all the other ' publick demonstrations of joy, as ringing of bells, store of bonefires '.[3]

The next three years are especially barren of records. Two sons of Henry Purcell, Thomas and Henry, died, and a daughter, Frances, was born. Daniel, his brother, was appointed organist of Magdalen College, Oxford, in 1688. But apart from the regular Birthday Odes, anthems, and one or two dramatic works of a tentative nature no detail of biographical interest remains of these years. Musically 1688 was one of the turning-points of Purcell's life, for it was in the autumn of this year that *Dido and Aeneas* was performed at Mr. Priest's school. How far this production affected Purcell's credit with the leaders of the literary and social world it is impossible to determine, and the operatic importance of the work must be left for later discussion.

In April 1689 Purcell had his famous quarrel with the Dean and Chapter of Westminster. It seems that, for certain remuneration, he introduced some people into the organ-loft to see the Coronation of William and Mary. The authorities apparently looked upon this money as their perquisite and—

' ordered that Mr. Purcell the organist to ye Deane & Chapter of Westminster doe pay to the hand of Mr. John Nedham Receiver of the Collegiate Church all such money as was received by him for places in the Organ Loft at ye Coronation

---

[1] Grove, *Dictionary*.   [2] *King's Musick*, 372.   [3] Luttrell.

of King William & Queen Mary by or before Saturday next being ye 20th day of this instant April. And in default thereof his place is declared to be null and void. And it is further ordered that his stipend or sallary due at our Lady(s) Day last past be detayned in the hands of the Treasurer untill further orders.' [1]

The pressure was too strong and Purcell paid over the money. In September of this year his youngest and only surviving son, Edward, was baptized in Westminster Abbey.

From now till the end of his life Purcell steadily wrote music for the theatre. Since his earliest essay in dramatic composition, *Theodosius*, he had provided music for some ten plays; but in some of these the only music was a dance, a couple of songs, or at most a short musical scene. Of these eleven plays with music, written in a space of eight years, only the last was of more than usual musical interest; and that was the amateurly produced *Dido and Aeneas*. From 1690 till his death five years later Purcell wrote music for no less than forty-four plays. None of these were in the modern sense of the word real operas: *Dido and Aeneas* was a freak experiment; but four were of such a scale as to be counted operas in the Dryden sense,[2] and four contain enough music to merit their being classed as musical plays.

In 1690 Purcell came into touch with Dryden through the admirable music he had written for the successful play *Dioclesian*. He was at once engaged to compose music for the Poet Laureate's farce *Amphitryon*, and the songs were published with the book of the play. In an introductory letter Dryden actually admitted his indebtedness to the composer,[3] and though till recently he had been a hot supporter of Grabu, the foreign Master of Music, he backed his new opinion by asking Purcell to write the music for his great patriotic play *King Arthur*, which was produced with great applause in the follow-

[1] Westminster Records.   [2] See p. 75 seq.   [3] See p. 76.

ing year. Purcell had by now considerable experience of dramatic composition, and in 1692 produced his masterpiece *The Fairy Queen.*

This same year Purcell apparently left the house in Bowling Alley East,[1] where he had lived since 1684, for this house and its neighbour now became assessed to one Ann Peters—a relative of Frances Purcell, no doubt. By 1693 he had moved again to a house in Marsham St., and it was perhaps from there that Roger Herbert wrote to the Earl of Rutland, ' I am now with Dr. Blow, Mr. Purcell, and some other great masters of musick ' (14 Oct.).[2] Roger Herbert's letter is very instructive with regard to the heartless way in which musicians were treated at the time : a German organist, Alberrix [Albrigi], was recommended by Blow to the Earl as being worth £100 a year, in spite of being a Roman Catholic ; but Herbert with great triumph reports to his noble patron that he has managed to beat the man down to £20. No wonder Purcell was not content with one office and a single fee !

At the end of the year Purcell, whose daughter, Mary Peters, was baptized on 10 Dec., resigned his post as organist at the Abbey and was succeeded by Dr. Blow. In 1694 he provided music for nine plays : not that this was the full extent of his output : in the same year he wrote his usual Royal Birthday Ode, composed a *Te Deum* and *Jubilate* with full orchestral accompaniment for St. Cecilia's Day, had his Centenary Ode performed at Trinity College, Dublin, was responsible for a whole concert of works performed ' At the consort-room in York-buildings . . . at the usual hour . . . for

[1] Now part of Tufton St. Purcell paid 14s. rates for the house in Bowling Alley from 1686 to 1691, and paid 14s. rates for a house in 1685 ; in 1684 he paid 10s. 6d., leaving 3s. 6d. in arrears, being marked in the margin ' gone ' ; so he probably moved from Great St. Ann's Lane to Bowling Alley at the end of 1684.

[2] Rowland MSS.

the entertainment of his Highness Prince Lewis of Baden ',[1] and revised and largely re-wrote for its twelfth edition Playford's book, *Introduction to the Skill of Musick*.

The year 1695 began for Purcell with two elegies and an anthem for the late queen : he wrote the music for seven more plays, composed a Birthday Ode for the small Duke of Gloucester, Princess Anne's son, and on 21 Nov. ' died Harry Purcell, our famous composer of music '.[2] He was buried in the north aisle of Westminster Abbey ' in a magnificent manner '[3] on 26 Nov. On the very day of his death he made his will :

> In the name of God Amen.
> I Henry Purcell of the Citty of Westminster gent., being dangerously ill as to the constitution of my body but in good and perfect mind and memory (thanks be to God) doe by these presents publish and declare this to be my last Will and Testament And I doe hereby give and bequeath unto my loveing wife ffrances Purcell all my Estate both reall and personall of what nature & kind soever to her and to her Assignes for ever And I doe hereby constitute and appoint my said loveing wife my sole Executrix of this my last Will and Testament revokeing all former Will or Wills. Witnesse my hand and seale this twentieth first day of November Annoque domini one thousand six hundred ninety five And in the seventh yeare of the Reigne of King William the third &c. H. Purcell.
> Signed sealed published and declared by the said Henry Purcell in the presence of W^m. Ecles John Chaplin, B: Peters. Proved 7th December, 1695, by the oath of Ffrances Purcell the relict & executrix.

A memorial cantata was composed by Jeremiah Clark ' (when organist at Winchester Colledge) upon ye Death of ye Famous

---

[1] *Gazette*, 25 Jan. 1694, No. 2,943 ; Hawkins, v. 5.
[2] Richard Powys to Matthew Prior, Marq. of Bath MSS.
[3] *Post Boy* for this date.

Mr Henry Purcell, and perform'd upon ye stage in Drury lane play house ' with chorus, orchestra and dances.[1]

Early in the following year Mrs. Purcell went to live in Dean's Yard [2] and from there published a few representative pieces of her husband's work, *Lessons for the Harpsichord, Sonatas in IV Parts, Ayres for the Theatre*, and some of his songs in a collection called *Orpheus Britannicus*, which was issued in two parts and achieved three editions. Mrs. Purcell died in 1706. Daniel, who had left Oxford for London at his brother's death and who won some momentary fame, died in 1717, leaving as sole legatee his ' natural and lawful brother ', Joseph.[3] Their uncle Edward died in the same year, and with the death of Henry Purcell's son Edward in 1740 [4] and his grandson, Edward Henry, organist of the Parish Church of Hackney from 22 Sept. 1753 to 3 Aug. 1755,[5] at a salary of £20, all trace of the composer's family is lost.

The only known portraits of Henry Purcell are : the Kneller drawing (Brit. Mus.), the head reproduced in this book, the *Sonnatas of 3 parts* engraving (1683) and the original of the Closterman frontispiece to *Orpheus Britannicus* (National Gallery).

For the next eighty years his fame as a musician was forgotten, except on paper—indeed from the day of his death Arne was perhaps the only serious musician who attempted to revive his

[1] Add. MS. 30934.

[2] The Rate-Books do not show Mrs. Purcell paying rates for a house in Dean's Yard in 1696 and 1697. Rates on the Mersham St. house were paid by her in 1695 and up to Easter 1696. Probably she lodged or stayed with a friend in Dean's Yard.

[3] P.C.C. Administration : 17 Jan. 1717/18.

[4] Grant of administration to his son 16 Oct. 1746.

[5] The Churchwarden gave notice of the vacancy on 3 Aug. : the previous meeting took place on 14 July, so presumably the death occurred between these dates.

music, apart from an ignorant editor or two—and the Purcell Club which was founded in 1836 did not last thirty years. It was not till 1876 and the foundation of the Purcell Society that he was remembered at all except for two or three songs ; but this new society set out bravely to publish all his music. In the seventeenth century his published works numbered less than a dozen : the eighteenth printed various selections such as *The Beauties of Purcell,* and in the nineteenth the Musical Antiquarian Society and Vincent Novello did their best. Now in 1927, though some thirty folio volumes have been issued, this monumental library edition is still unfinished and already discrepancies have been found in the earlier volumes. But Henry Purcell is at last being considered at his proper value—a value far higher than the formal dictionary praise which has always, curiously enough, been awarded him : he was undoubtedly a master in his art, and that by the age of thirty-six. Indeed it is possible that if he ' had been blest with long life, we might have had a music of our own at least as good as that of France or Germany '.[1]

2

Sacred Music

PURCELL has been perhaps more misunderstood in his sacred music than in any other branch of his compositions. At first sight Sir Hubert Parry's strictures [2] are justified.

' The taste of the age is obviously predominant, tempered at times by flashes of sincere genius. The most universal fact which strikes anyone who thinks about it, is the extravagant extent to which Purcell's work of this kind differed from the old devotional church music. That had been essentially choral, representing the direct expression of

[1] Burney. [2] *Oxford History of Music,* iii, pp. 278 sqq.

devotional feeling by human beings. . . . It looks as though
the choral portions of anthems had fallen so completely into
disfavour with the church public that they had shrivelled
up into the meanest and most insignificant proportions, and
were pushed into a corner at the end of the anthem to
accompany the shuffling of the feet while people were pre-
paring to kneel down again after their musical entertainment. . . . The mature anthems of Purcell . . . contain
a larger amount of purely instrumental music than is to be
found in almost any period of English church music [and
this] could only have come into use through concession to
predominating taste, which was led to a great extent by the
King himself.'

That Charles II was in part responsible for these instrumental interpolations is borne out by Tudway :

' His Majesty, who was a brisk and airy Prince, coming to
ye Crown in ye flow'r and vigour of his Age, was soon,
if I may so say, tyred wth ye grave and solemn way, and
ordered ye Composers of his Chappell to add Symphonys,
&c., with Instruments to their Anthems, and thereupon
established a select number of his Private Musick to play y^e
Symphonys and Ritornelles which he had appointed. The
King did not intend by this innovation to alter anything
of the established way. He only appointed this to be done
when he came himself to ye Chappell, which was only upon
Sundays, on ye Mornings of ye Great Festivals and Days of
Offerings.'

The King, according to Roger North, ' could not bear any
musick to which he could not keep the time, and that he
constantly did to all that was presented to him '. But it would
be quite as absurd to consider Purcell's instrumental ritornelli
irreligious as to regard polyphony as a religious medium only.
The false and arbitrary division between secular and sacred
music which has obtained since the Victorian age would at that
time have been considered inexplicable. God could be praised

' in the cymbals and dancing ' and sacred joy differed but little from human enthusiasm.

Parry, it seems, regarded melody as irreligious, for he praises Purcell and his contemporaries in that the solo music in their anthems

> ' has no pretensions whatever to tunefulness. One would almost think composers made up their minds that, whatever concessions they had to make to popular taste, there was a point below which they could not demean themselves. And it cannot be denied that, in view of the great facility of Purcell and some of his contemporaries in composing tuneful ditties, it is very surprising and noteworthy that they never bring their abilities in that direction to bear in church music . . . which is very much to their credit.'

It seems amazing that melody, which should be the foundation of all music, should be regarded as irreligious ; besides, it is untrue that Purcell omitted tunefulness from his church music. That he did not fill his anthems with jig-tunes would only be surprising if he had had no mentality.

The complaint that the choral parts were ' pushed into a corner ' cannot be brought home to Purcell. He was by no means eager to depend on soloists alone, but he was sensible enough to be willing to make the best of any circumstances that might arise. When he began composing for the church, the country at large and the conditions of music in particular were not yet righted. The rebellion had not only destroyed a vast amount of church music, but had scattered the choirs. Large choral services had been anathema during the Commonwealth and only four organ-builders remained in England. At the Restoration Bernhardt Schmidt—' Father ' Smith, after his adoption into this country—and Renatus Harris were invited to put up new organs all over England. The choirs had been so depleted that—

> ' For above a year after the opening of His Majesty's

Chappel the orderers of the Musick there, were necessitated to supply superior parts of the music with cornets, and men's feigned voices, there being not one lad for all that time capable of singing his part readily.' [1]

When Purcell went to Westminster he was fortunate in finding a good choir but no organ : he therefore wrote anthems for the Abbey in four, five, six, and eight parts. At the Chapel Royal, however, owing perhaps to the temporary dissolution of the choir, he found only twelve boys—who possibly were not as yet reliable—and he was obliged to write for the brilliant men's voices alone, employing only a minimum of chorus at the points of climax. This depletion of the choirs may have had no less to do with the introduction of instrumental sections than the taste of the King, for a series of solos, duets, and trios, unrelieved by choral sections, would be intolerable without some instrumental break : as it is, Purcell is at times hard put to it to avoid monotony in anthems of this type. To our ears the introduction of violins in the place of the cornet was an admirable innovation, but Evelyn laments this

'concert of 24 violins betweene every pause, after yᵉ French fantastical light way, better suiting a tavern, or a play-house, than a church. This was yᵉ first time of change, and now we no more hear the cornet wᶜʰ gave life to yᵉ organ ; that instrument quite left off, in which the English were so skilful.' [2]

This innovation, coupled with an advance in harmonic outlook, must have been doubly surprising ; for, although church music had to all intents stopped during the Commonwealth, musicians were developing their technique in private— indeed the number of text-books on music published during the interregnum is remarkable—and the progress that had been

[1] *Present Practice of Music Vindicated*, Matthew Locke, 1673.
[2] *Diary*, 21 Dec. 1662.

made would, for most people, have been unrealized until the results were suddenly presented after the Restoration. Purcell was even more advanced in style than most of his contemporaries. Dr. Blow, it is true, is bold, but his boldness is shown by an occasional venture into the harmonic regions where the Elizabethans were unafraid and where Purcell revelled. He had neither the skill nor the love for the flights of dramatic intensity and pictorial realism which his brilliant pupil essayed. It is very tempting to quote at length examples of Purcell's masterly strokes of realism—his settings of ' joy ', ' pain ', ' deep ', ' swift ', his shrewd touches that imply or imitate a trumpet, walking, sleeping, melting, even knitting. At times his settings are merely pictorial, and such examples could only be given to show his consummate skill in realistic music, but it is seldom that he loses sight of the greater beauty of pure music, and for the most part, as will be seen from the examples given, the realism is entirely incidental and the beauty the beauty of absolute music.

His dramatic sense was very strong, and he could not resist turning into music the least suggestion of mood or motion. Such expressions as ' endureth ', ' steadfast ', and ' fixed ' are set to long notes to imply a rock-like firmness, often contrasted with moving parts in the other voices or in the accompaniment. Even when the words are metaphorical they are set according to their literal sense : ' For though the Lord be high, yet hath He respect unto the lowly,' in the anthem *I will give thanks unto Thee, O Lord*, is set with a high note on the word ' high ' followed by a falling passage that extends down through two octaves and a note, finishing on the bass's low D. This is perhaps somewhat extravagant, but it is in fact only a development of the sense which makes a good composer avoid setting ' That can sing both high and low ' as if the line ended ' both low and high '. At times this scrupulous attention to detail seems pedantic or even grotesque, but when, as in almost every example, this love of literal translation is merely incidental, the effect is rather of a strong vitality and personality.

Burney is especially enthusiastic on the subject of Purcell's anthems, which he says were always ' heard with pious rapture wherever they could be performed '. In his opinion Purcell was as successful in the elaborate and learned style of Tallis, Byrd, and Gibbons—that is, in fugue, imitation, or plain counterpoint, with organ accompaniment—as in the newer and more expressive style, so full of feeling and imagination, with the orchestral accompaniment of which he was one of the principal inventors. Burney states that Purcell's genius can only be appreciated by those who understand the state of music before his time, ' compared with which, his productions for the Church, if not more learned, will be found infinitely more varied and expressive '. It is perhaps true that only those who have some knowledge of the development of music in general and of church music in particular can hope to appreciate to the full these anthems and services, though—to judge from Parry—they may be misunderstood. It is said that no admirer of Elizabethan drama can approve of Restoration plays to any extent, and the same may be true of the music ; but a great number of Purcell's anthems must inevitably strike musicians and all who hear them sung as works which, if they fall short of true greatness, are but little less than works of genius.

Until more is known of Purcell's development in musical style it is impossible to draw from his anthems any definite conclusions about his church music, as the chronology of the works is so vague. Of some sixty-five anthems only forty-one can be dated and of these only ten are certain.[1] Since Mr.

---

[1] Of these nine are dated in the manuscript by John Gostling, the famous bass who sang so many of the solos in the anthems. Seventeen others can be put down as dating earlier than 1683, from the fact that they occur in

Barclay Squire's invaluable examination of the chronology of the dramatic music [1] it seems probable that it is by a critical study of the dramatic music that light will be thrown on the development of Purcell's style and so on the chronology of the anthems. Till this is done it is impossible to do more than make a vague study of the church music in general, and one must be satisfied with a close criticism of each anthem individually.

It is not surprising that the early anthems are apparently those which are chiefly contrapuntal and which include few solos. Not only was there a good full choir at Westminster with perhaps little opportunity of finding strings in the place of the non-existent organ, but Purcell was besides fresh from his job of copyist. From his appointment to that office in 1676 to the time when, four years later, he took over the duties of organist at the Abbey from Dr. Blow, he had been engaged in transcribing copy after copy of anthems by all the leading Elizabethan composers and their immediate successors. He must have gained by this—even if he had not already learned it from the Chapel Royal masters—a thorough grounding in contrapuntal technique, and it is but natural that his first essays in sacred music should be written in this medium. *Hear my prayer* (in eight parts), *Jehovah, quam multi sunt hostes* (in five parts with solos for tenor and bass), *O God, Thou hast cast us out* (in six parts), and *O Lord God of hosts* (in eight parts) are all fine, straightforward works in the true Elizabethan tradition.

The last two were a great source of worry to Dr. Burney. The first movement seemed to him elaborate, yet spirited and pleasing, and the verse ' O be Thou our help ' contained some new and fine effects : ' The unprepared 7th in the second and sixth bar was here, I believe, used for the first time. With the

the two manuscript books in the Fitzwilliam Museum at Cambridge, which bear the dates 1682 and 1683.

[1] *Sammelbände der Internationalen Musik-Gesellschaft*, 1903–4.

last movement I should be much more pleased if the sharp 3rd and flat 6th did not so frequently occur.' The poor doctor found this chord particularly hard to accept : it occurs three times in *O Lord God of hosts* ' and to my ear seems jarring '. The first movement of this anthem Burney describes as ' a noble composition, *alla Palestrina* ', in which all the laws of fugue upon two and sometimes more subjects is preserved inviolate : the harmony, though bold, is ' chaste ', and the whole effect spirited and majestic. The second movement is extremely pathetic and expressive, but, as in the last movement, there are experiments in harmony that ' give the ear more pain than pleasure '—a fact all the more to be deplored because Purcell is so classical a church composer that his harmonic licences ' may lead young students into error ' : chords of the 13th in particular, says the doctor, ' affect me always with the idea of wrong notes in the performance '. But apart from these blemishes Burney considered this anthem to be one of the finest compositions of any church. It is indeed an excellent work ; the counterpoint is admirable, the harmonic ' licences ' to-day seem expressive, and the realistic touches—such as the brilliantly suggestive but not blatant setting of the word ' laugh ' and the following quotation—

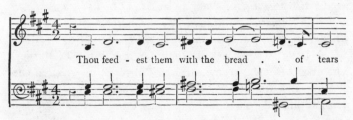

give a life and colour to the whole which are all the more remarkable when it is remembered that this anthem was written before the composer was twenty-four years of age.

Purcell could get the right effect by the simplest means. He could also remain a musician while using the most extravagant splashes of sound. His early anthem *Let God arise*, no doubt a choir-boy effort, is an unpretentious simple composition that rings true because of its clean sincerity and lack of striving. So too in *Jehovah, quam multi sunt hostes*, which is perhaps Purcell's most beautiful work in the Elizabethan manner, the words ' Voce mea ad Jehovam clamanti ' are perfectly set with the surging rise of all the voices and the sudden inspiration of the minor chord on the word ' clamanti '.

In the well-known, most expressive anthem *My beloved spake*— also in all probability an early work—it is again the slightest touch that makes the greatest effect : the clash of harmonies on the last words of the line ' and the voice of the turtle is heard in our land ' has exactly caught the murmuring of the doves,

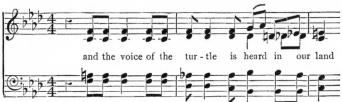

but on paper—and still more on the piano—this seems so impossible that editors have obstinately ' improved ' on Purcell with some Victorian insipidity.

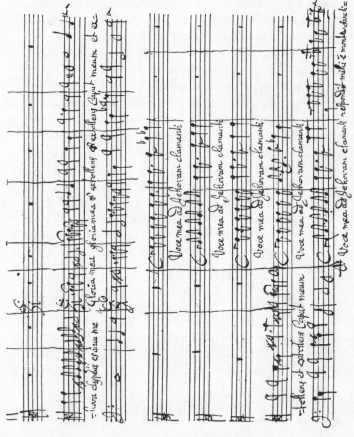

II. Part of the motet *Jehovah, quam multi sunt hostes* (see p. 35) in the autograph of Henry Purcell, Add. MS. 30930.

So easy is it for the unwary and the cowards to disbelieve
or fight shy of some of Purcell's braveries that it is a pleasure to
find an anthem that cannot offend their prejudices or sus-
picions. Yet even in the short five-part anthem *Remember not,
Lord,* which is particularly simple in style, very easy to sing,
and exceedingly moving with its sense of humble confession—
even here Parry finds a harmonic gnat ready to be strained at :
he labels certain consecutive sevenths as a device to attract the
attention of the worshippers, employed in place of the earlier
attempt to put them into ' the trance-like sleep of devotional
ecstasy '.[1] He does not go so far as to approve the earlier
custom of inducing trance-like sleeps, but he apparently regards
the sevenths as an harmonic trick, quite forgetting that in his
additions to Playford's *Skill of Musick* Purcell accepts

> ' taking two *Sevenths* together in whatsoever *Key* you shall
> Compose in, with this Allowance, that two *Major Sevenths*
> together is not good, but two *Minor Sevenths* together is
> allowable : Also, if you take two *Sevenths*, so the one be
> *Minor* and the other *Major*, it is allow'd, but be sure the
> *Minor* be set before the *Major*, as you see in the Example.'

This may seem a daring rule or permission, but Purcell's
qualification about the Minor Seventh preceding the Major
is at least common sense according to all accepted ideas of
melodic progression from the time of *musica ficta*, and this
anyway shows that consecutive sevenths—in Purcell's hands,
if not in those of his contemporaries or of twentieth-century

[1] *Oxford History*, 274.

composers—were not employed as a trick to catch the attention of the audience or of the congregation.

Parry seems so prejudiced against the church music of the Restoration that there is little temptation to agree with any of his opinions on the subject : he seems to have totally misunderstood the period. But in one criticism he makes on Purcell's anthems most musicians of to-day will agree. He greatly deplores ' the gabbling " hallelujahs " which are of such frequent and distressing occurrence at the end of the Restoration anthems. The intention is apparently to suggest the eager and joyful acclamation of the " blessed ", but the result is nearly always trivial.' To us indeed—who for the most part have to judge by the printed page—the result is little short of the trivial. But it must be remembered that often the baldest effects on paper become electrically brilliant when sung, and we are besides biased by the undeniable fact that we do not think as the seventeenth century thought. To us the gabbled hallelujahs in the anthems *Behold, I bring* ; *In Thee, O Lord* ; *It is a good thing* ; *Why do the heathen*, and *Thy way, O God* seem fatuous. To congregations of the time they did not seem fatuous, and it may well be that our sophistication has brought with it a lack of simplicity which is rather a loss to us than an achievement that warrants any self-congratulation. Dr. Burney indeed found the quick parts of the last anthem ' somewhat *passés*, and the melody to these words, " the air thundered," &c. seems too light and dramatic for the church at any period ', but the music in the slow parts was still excellent for him.

It is not to be expected that all the anthems are brilliant. Some are merely ordinary : others, such as *I will sing unto the Lord* and *The Lord is King* with its tedious bass solos, are merely bald and dull. *The way of God*—one of his last works for the church—is surprisingly meaningless : the bass is for the most part a constant succession of subdominant followed by tonic, pointless figures are given to the second syllable of the word ' unto '—an amazing lapse from Purcell's usually scrupulous attention to accentuation ; and the elaborate cross rhythms at the end merely accentuate the banality of the whole. The unnecessary roulades on the word ' unto ' are nothing but examples of virtuosity as opposed to ornamentation. The dividing line is indeed remarkably difficult to gauge. *O Lord, Thou art my God* is full of coloratura passages, but there they are set to words such as ' wonderful ', ' spread ', ' glad ', and ' allelujah ', where there is excuse enough for figuration. In the anthem *My song shall be alway*, however, ' wondrous ', ' raging ', and ' arise ' (curiously again the first syllable) are not the only words for which roulades are used ; such unsuitable words as ' generation ' and ' habitation ' are treated with four- and two-bar virtuoso passages : but this work was obviously written especially for some brilliant mezzo-soprano singer,[1] as it is one long solo relieved for seven short bars in the middle and at the end by a chorus of four parts.

One of Purcell's greatest anthems—' an elaborate and fine composition ' Burney calls it—was performed at the coronation of James II on 23 April 1685.

' The QUEEN being thus ANOINTED and CROWNED, and having received all *Her Royal Ornaments*, the *Choirs* sang the following *Verse-Anthem*, performed by the whole *Consort of Voices* and *Instruments*. | Anthem IX | Psalm 45, Vers. 1 : " *My Heart is Inditing of a good Matter* " (&c). As soon as this *Anthem* began, the QUEEN arose from Her *Faldstool*, and, being supported by the Two *Bishops*, and Her Train born, and attended as before, went up to the *Theatre ;* and as She approached towards the KING, bowed Her Self rever-

---

[1] It is perhaps fantastic to imagine the singer to have been young Bowen, the boy for whom Purcell later wrote the dully virtuoso setting of the song in *The Massacre of Paris.*

ently to His MAJESTY sitting upon *His Throne ;* and so was Conducted to Her Own THRONE on the Left Hand of the KING, where *She* reposed Her Self till the *Anthem* was ended.' [1]

This anthem was written for eight voices—two trebles and a mezzo-soprano, alto, tenor, baritone, and two basses—with string accompaniment. The instrumental introduction or Symphony is a fine, typical example : it is in two movements, the first a majestic march with a steady rhythmic pulse of two minims in the bar, followed by a longer triple-time movement in fugal style. This is immediately followed by fugal entries of the chorus in the same rhythm for some thirty bars with a short instrumental ritornello as a coda. The time now changes to two minims in the bar for the lines ' At his right hand shall stand the queen all glorious within, her clothing is of wrought gold ' : this too is treated fugally, but is given more brilliance by the figures with which the word ' glorious ' is decorated. The key of the anthem—C major—is now left and a long verse in six and seven parts, passing through the keys of E minor, B minor, A minor, C minor, D minor, F major, and G minor, prepares for the fine chorus ' With joy and gladness shall they be brought '. This chorus, like the preceding verse, is in triple time, and also depends for its effect on mass writing broken up by answering bursts of sound from voices or strings : the whole of this magnificent movement is characterized by Purcell's usual ' joy ' idiom—

Str.

[1] Sandford's *History of the Coronation of James II*, p. 101.

and ends with a grand rhythmic phrase which is perilously near Parry's tuneful secularities—

After a repetition of the whole introductory Symphony there comes a verse in eight and six parts—'Hearken, O daughter, consider'—chiefly in A minor and again full of answering phrases from different combinations of the voices. A short, tuneful ritornello for the strings ends this section, and there

follows a miraculous paean of joy from the full chorus ' Praise
the Lord, O Jerusalem '—

again a short instrumental ritornello and the whole stupendous
work is brought to a close by an amazing allelujah chorus.
This last movement is perhaps the most brilliant section of the
whole anthem. The splendid vigour of the opening theme,

bound together by the strong amens, with the sense of renewed
joy implied by the change from B natural to B flat is heightened
by the swelling, surging, bell-like peals of sound that follow—

and the climax is reached in the last eight short bars in which
the insistent cries of allelujah must be recognized as the
inevitable and overwhelming end to a truly great work of
musical genius.

Al - le - lu - ia, al - le - lu - ia, al - le -

- lu - ia, al - le - lu - ia, al - le - lu - ia, al - le -

- lu - - - - ia.

I have examined this anthem fairly closely as it is perhaps the grandest of Purcell's compositions for the church. *Praise the Lord, O my soul, O Lord* is almost as magnificent, but it is not so grandly conceived. By far the most beautiful anthem with solos and choruses is *O sing unto the Lord*. This 'long and elaborate work'[1] is filled with melody: the allelujahs at the

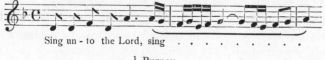

Sing un - to the Lord, sing . . . .

[1] Burney.

beginning with the answering strings, the charming quartet
' Sing unto the Lord ' with its Bach-like subject, the short choral
acclamation 'Glory and worship are before Him ', the reverent
verse and chorus ' O worship the Lord ' and especially the
superb bass solo and chorus ' Tell it out among the heathen
that the Lord is King ' are wonderful parts of a splendid work

which, if only because of the mastery of melodic line displayed
all through, tends to make Handel stolid and dull in comparison,
or at least exposes him as a clever imitator.

Be merciful unto me, a late composition with a fine bass solo,
is an excellent work which almost merits Burney's enthusiastic
praises : ' Indeed, to my conceptions, there seems no better
Music existing, of the kind, than the opening of this anthem,
in which the verse, " I will praise God ", and the last movement, in C natural, are in melody, harmony, and modulation,
truly *divine Music.*' It is unusual for Dr. Burney to include

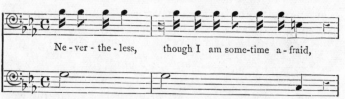

Ne-ver-the-less,   though I am some-time a-fraid,

(From *Be merciful unto me.*)

Purcell's harmony among the praiseworthy characteristics of the composer. If only ' the sharp 3rd and flat 6th did not so frequently occur ', perhaps the other licences could have been swallowed with a tolerable grace. The anthem *O God, Thou art my God*, comes in for a fair amount of pained criticism: this work must have been the product of Purcell's youth

> ' before he had refined his ear, or exercised his judgment ; as there are many crude harmonies, and false accents in it, which in riper years he would not have tolerated. . . . Line III, bar 3, the E♮ in the tenor part with F and G, immediately preceding a close in F, has a very disagreeable effect (*a*). C would be better harmony; but then the point of imitation would not be so complete.[1] The 6th with the 7th, in the next bar, is hardly defensible (*b*) —

. . . In the next page he has the 6th with the 7th, and flat 3rd, 4th, and 5th, again ; which last combination, though

---

[1] Purcell was exceptionally brave in his logic where points of imitation were concerned : a more striking example can be seen in the anthem, *Praise the Lord, O Jerusalem*—the fugal passage, ' So will we sing and praise Thy pow'r '.

he had authority from old masters, no composers, since his time, seem to have admitted into their works. P. 150, the sharp 5th to E♭ must have been thought very licentious, during the last century; yet, as a note of taste, it has a good effect, and as such, is now frequently used. The harmony throughout the last movement, in triple time, is piquant, and the modulation agreeable, though the close in A is very extraneous. The *hallelujah* is in all respects, the use of the sharp 3rd with the flat 6th excepted, extremely agreeable.'

From these regretful strictures an impression might be formed that Purcell's anthems are mere conglomerations of more or less harmful discords. Yet many of them are characterized by their clean, sharp-cut simplicity. Some have already been quoted. Others are, *Out of the deep*, *Why do the heathen*, with its fine treatment of the instruments that accompany the voices, and the grand, blameless work, *O praise God*. The last two only are mentioned by Burney, and then are merely catalogued as being in Purcell's manuscript in the Royal Collection. *O praise God* should have been examined more closely by Burney, that he might have found a work free from most of his pet harmonic objections, and Parry should have remembered this anthem before he wrote his sweeping statement about tunefulness. The instrumental introduction, with its swinging rhythm, is as good a tune as any in the dramatic music of the period, and is far more suitable to the spirit of the whole anthem than the diluted essence of insipid purity or the supreme dullness of earnest worth with which the so-called religious music of the nineteenth century was coloured. Play over this instrumental introduction, then listen to the voices that Purcell added to this introduction, and then consider whether the religion of the seventeenth century as reflected in such music as this was not every whit as careful and immeasurably more genuine and natural than ours of to-day.

ALTO,
TENOR,
AND
TWO
BASSES.

O praise God, praise God in his ho - li - ness,

STR.

O praise God, praise God in his ho - li - ness.

Besides writing some sixty anthems for the Church, Purcell also composed three services—in G minor, in B flat major, and in D major. The G minor service only deserves to be remembered as having played a part in the story of Novello and the copyist,[1] but the B flat service, though an early work —as can be seen by a study of the word-accents— is, as Burney says, ' most agreeable '. The service comprises settings for the Morning, Communion, Evening services with the *Benedicite*, *Jubilate*, *Cantate*, and *Deus Misereatur*. Burney praises the whole work, and even approves some unexpected but stimulating modulations that surprisingly did not give his ear the least uneasiness ; but he still boggles at that sharp 3rd and flat 6th and the flat 3rd, 4th, and 5th, ' which, I hope, in spite of my reverence for Purcell, the organists of our cathedrals scruple not to change for better harmony '. Unfortunately, organists and editors have been only too eager to comply, and the task of scraping away their light green paint is none too easy. But a certain sympathy is due to the honest doctor. He was quite ready to learn and quite acquiescent at the suggestion that he should swallow new harmonies if they were suitably surrounded with good homely fare.

' The ear will patiently bear very rough usage from an artist who in general makes it such ample amends ; however, there are limits, beyond which it is unsafe to exercise cruelty of all kinds ; and the auricular sense will be deadened, disgusted, or rendered indifferent to Music's powers, by too harsh treatment.'

All the B flat settings are simple. For the most part the words are set with no repetitions, and generally the writing is

[1] In 1828 a copyist asked for five weeks in which to copy this service and four anthems at York : Novello had already done the job in two days : the originals were burnt with the Choir of the Minster in the following February.

in blocks, with occasional points of imitation and moments of
relief given by the contrast of verse and full, with trios alternat-
ing between the upper three parts and the lower voices.
Purcell has here damped his dramatic exuberance—practically
limiting his power of tone-painting to the words, ' To give
light to them that sit in darkness, and in the shadow of death '
and ' He hath scattered the proud '. Indeed the whole cycle
of services appears to consist of thoroughly capable exercises
in technique which cannot be accused of academicism because
of the predominance of musical ideas. The whole work well
repays close study, if only because Purcell ' had the patience,
as well as the abilities, to enrich it with no less than four
different canons of the most difficult construction, as of 2, 3,
and 4 in one, by inversion '. There are, in fact, nine canons
to bear witness to the composer's skill—the *Gloria* in the
Deus Misereatur being one of the finest examples of a 4 in 1
canon, according to Horsley.[1] But, quite apart from the
ingenuity displayed, these services are, if not great, excellent
examples of sound work—for all that Burney finds a line in the
Magnificat so full of exceptionable combinations that he ' cannot
pass it over without a stigma '.

But if the B flat services can be dismissed as admirably
sound musical exercises, a very different judgement must be
given to the D major *Te Deum and Jubilate*. This magnificent
work for five-part chorus, solo voices, strings, trumpets, and
organ was ' Made for St. Cecilia's Day, 1694 ',[2] for performance
by the Musical Society, and

> ' The Pains he bestow'd in preparing it for so Great and
> Judicious an Auditory were highly rewarded by their kind

[1] *Canons of Various Species.*

[2] According to Mrs. Purcell in the published copy. Tudway says it was
written for the opening of St. Paul's, but the first part of the new Cathedral
—the Choir—was not opened till 1697.

Reception of it when it was first Perform'd, and more yet by their Intention to have it repeated at their *Annual Meeting*'.[1]

Dr. Burney's criticism of this work is so admirable that I must quote his opinions at length, rather than attempt to convey the same impressions in less picturesque language. A short introduction sets a triumphant tone for the opening trio which ushers in the full chorus on the words ' All, all the earth doth worship Thee, the Father everlasting '. The brilliant opening of this chorus with the beautiful effect of the ascending part-writing and the richness of the harmony and counterpoint in the joyful setting of the word ' everlasting ' is admirably contrasted with the sudden quiet of the succeeding passage. ' But it seems to me as if *all* the composers of this hymn had mistaken the cry of *joy* for that of *sorrow*, in setting *To thee all angels cry aloud*.' Purcell, like Handel, sets this line admirably, but unsuitably, in the minor. The Cherubim and Seraphim sing in two parts, and the acclamation of the whole chorus of the word ' Holy ' is excellently inspired. The sudden drop to a solo bass voice on the words ' and earth ' is to-day rather ridiculous, but these two bars are amply compensated for by the grandeur of the chorus, ' are full of the Majesty of Thy Glory'. ' The transient state of melody has, however, rendered this verse " The glorious company of the Apostles praise thee ", and, indeed, most of the solo parts, somewhat rude and inelegant.' I would go further than the doctor and say that the three solo laudations with their coloratura passages are tedious : in Sir Frederick Bridge's excellent edition of the *Te Deum* some sixteen bars of roulade are bracketed for possible omission, but this, I am afraid, only scamps the difficulty without smoothing it away, as the result is very uneven and arhythmic. ' Also the Holy Ghost ', for two altos in triple time is a ' delightful fragment

[1] In the Dedication of the published copy, 1694.

of harmony and melody, which time can never injure '. The double fugue of ' Thou art the King of glory ', which is grand and masterly, is followed by a beautiful duet for alto and bass voices which is full of ' permanent beauties of melody, contrivance, and expression, that are wholly out of the reach of fashion '. Burney does not include the division on the word ' all ' in this praise, but to me it seems beautiful in itself and inevitable in the context.[1] Strangely, Burney's next object for praise and mine for blame is another division—that on the word ' glory ' in ' Thou sittest at the right hand of God, in the Glory of the Father ': this is set for two sopranos. The whole movement, ' O Lord, save Thy people ', is a poignant echo to the sense and the hope of the words ' Lift them up for ever ' is admirably expressed. After a short choral setting of ' Day by day we magnify Thee ', there comes an alto solo, ' Vouchsafe, O Lord ', of which the start is one of the most moving pieces of sacred music in existence. Burney could not say as much, for he only had the printed copies, and found them so vilely printed that it was impossible to

[1] A great difficulty in performance would be to find a singer capable of taking the alto solos ; the average male alto would be unbearable.

Lord, to keep us this day with-

- out sin, O

Lord, O Lord, have mer-cy, have

mer-cy,　　　have mer-cy up - on us,　　　have mer-cy,

mer - - - - - cy up - on　us.

know which notes were intended.　It is a tragedy that the
final fugue, 'Let me never be confounded', is so ordinary:
as Burney says, it might have been written by a lesser genius,
and is indeed a sad finish to a really great work.

The beginning of the *Jubilate* was evidently written to show
the powers of a fine performer, but Burney takes exception
at the military cast given by the pointed notes, as he 'never
was partial to that style of movement', and much regretted
the constant occurrence of such passages in Purcell and his
contemporaries.　'Be ye sure that the Lord' and the following movement must always be considered good music 'if
sung with taste and feeling'.　The verse 'For the Lord is

gracious' shows to the full Purcell's powers of expression, especially at the words 'his mercy is everlasting', which is exquisite. The *Gloria* is written *alla Palestrina,* but is more animated than any 'that Palestrina was allowed to compose'. It is so full of science and contrivance that only musicians can attempt to appreciate it to the full, but the whole work is so glorious and sublime 'as must charm into rapture the most ignorant, as well as the most learned hearer'; and the doctor adds an apologetic foot-note to the effect that this review is not meant to exalt Purcell at the expense of Handel.

This magnificent work, which deserves to be performed at every great festival, was constantly sung at St. Paul's at the feast of the Sons of the Clergy from 1695 to 1713, and also on great occasions of state when Queen Anne visited the cathedral. For the next thirty years it was performed alternately with Handel's Dettingen *Te Deum.* After 1743 it was seldom performed—even at the Three Choirs Festival—for

'Handel's superior knowledge and use of instruments, and more polished melody, and, indeed, the novelty of his productions, which, *caeteris paribus,* will always turn the public scale, took such full possession of the nation's favour, that Purcell's *Te Deum* is now only performed occasionally, as an antique curiosity, even in this country'.

Now that Handel has for so long been exalted at the expense of Purcell it is surely time to start turning the public scale, and the *Te Deum* is the work that could with ease turn it, though it should only be performed on festival occasions, when presumably the best voices and orchestras are available.

Apart from all these works that Purcell composed definitely for church use, there are his seventeen so-called hymns that were printed in the two volumes of Playford's *Harmonia Sacra.* Most of these are more or less dramatic recitatives without any definite rhythmic sections. Some have short rhythmic endings, five with a chorus of two or three parts. Twelve are for treble solo, two for bass solo, one for treble and bass, one for two basses, and one for treble, alto, and bass. The majority are, it must be confessed, rather tedious—very reminiscent of the translations from the classics and the paraphrases from the Bible that were coming into fashion. The words of five of the hymns are by Dr. William Fuller—Bishop of Lincoln, Dr. Taylor—Bishop of Down, and George Herbert, while ' Mr. Norris of Wadham Colledge, Oxon ' provided the words of three ; two were by Abraham Cowley, two by Nahum Tate, and one, the beautiful poem, *Upon a Quiet Conscience*, was ' *by King* Charles *the* I. *of Blessed Memory* '.

The finest of these works is *An Evening Hymn*, ' Now that the sun hath veil'd his light ', a calm and peaceful composition upon a ground for treble solo. In *Job's Curse*, Purcell has admirably caught the sad, melancholy atmosphere of the words, as he has in the setting of Herbert's poem, ' With sick and famish'd eyes '. *A Penitential Hymn* is a fine work, but unfortunately is damned for us by the distasteful words : lepers to-day can only be mentioned without details about their sores. *The Blessed Virgin's Expostulation* is a touching piece of dramatic recitative in which Purcell well portrays the pathetic anxiety of the Mother at the loss of her Son, ' When our Saviour (at Twelve Years of Age) had withdrawn himself '. *An Hymn upon the Last Day* is a vigorous work for two basses, which only differs in mood from, and is no less fine than, the short dramatic scene from the first Book of Samuel ' In guilty Night '. This musical setting of the visit of Saul to the Witch of Endor and the consequent raising of the ghost of Samuel is in fact the forerunner of the dramatic type of oratorio. The three voices begin with a description of the scene—short, but cleverly implying the dark mystery of Saul's visit. A long, vivid dialogue between the king and the witch follows, and

slowly Samuel's spirit rises to foretell Saul's sad fate. 'To-
morrow thou and thy son shall be with me beneath,' are the
last words of the prophet as he sinks down again into the
darkness, leaving Saul groaning at his approaching doom, while
the weird farewells of the witch and the vision she raised fade
away into the night.

After this exquisite miniature it is perhaps difficult to
appreciate the bigger works; but it is necessary to point out
a few short examples of Purcell's skill in tone-painting as
shown in the anthems, if only to prove that his dramatic

instinct was hardly ever allowed to swamp his musical taste. There is no need to dwell upon the low D to which he makes his bass soloist descend in going down to the sea in ships, nor on the delicate implication in the setting of ' So that the waves thereof are still ', where the swell is almost seen subsiding, nor on the two octave descent for the words ' Bow Thy heavens, O Lord, and come down ' (*Blessed be the Lord*), nor even on the amazing drops of a ninth in the setting of the words, ' But fall, but fall under my feet ', from the anthem, *The way of God*. But the poignant treatment of the words from the anthem, *Blessed is he that considereth*, ' The Lord comfort him when he lieth sick upon his bed ', must be quoted :

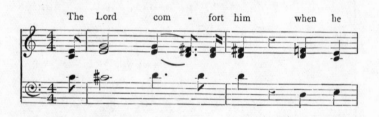

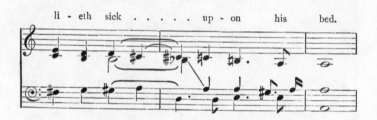

there is no need for comment, the skill and the real beauty is apparent enough even from the printed page. Two quotations must also be made from the funeral anthem, *Man that is born*.

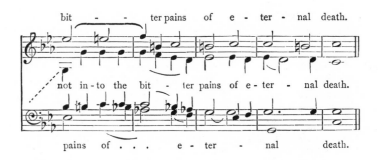

It is easy to appreciate the account given by Tudway [1] of the performance of this anthem at the funeral of Queen Mary in Westminster Abbey :

> ' A Great Queen, and extreamly lamented, being there to be interr'd, everybody present was disposed and serious at so solemn a service, as indeed they ought to be at all parts of divine Worship. I appeal to all that were present, as well such as understood Music, as those that did not, whether they ever heard anything so rapturously fine and solemn and so Heavenly in the Operation, which drew tears from all.'

When Croft printed his own setting of the Funeral Sentences (1724), he wrote in the preface :

> ' In that *Service* there is one *Verse* composed by my Predecessor, the Famous Mr. *Henry Purcell*, to which, in Justice to his Memory, his Name is applied ; the Reason why I did not compose that *Verse* a-new (so as to render the whole *Service* entirely of my own Composition), is obvious to every Artist ; in the rest of That *Service* composed by me, I have endeavoured, as near as possible I could, to imitate that great Master.'

There is one outstanding merit in all Purcell's music that has not yet been especially noticed : that is, his unerring

---

[1] In the preface to the fourth volume of his church music, re-punctuated for intelligibility by G. E. P. Arkwright, *Musical Antiquary*, i, p. 247.

instinct for correct word-accentuation. His earlier compositions are at times marred by inexact accent, but even here
he is never greatly at fault. All his later works are remarkable
for the most scrupulous attention to phrasing and stress. In
this respect a comparison of the *Te Deum* in B flat with that
in D is most instructive. 'We acknowledge Thee' is set to
long notes in the former : in the latter four quavers are enough
for the first four syllables. 'Continually', 'fellowship',
'keep us this day', are all set to shorter and quicker notes in
the later version.

A triple or double ending such as 'majesty', 'heritage',
'Father', or 'glory' was invariably set in the later works with
an accent on the first syllable only. In all the examples that
have been quoted Purcell's care of the word-accent can be
seen : in his recitatives he was untiring in his determination
to get the exact shade of stress if it was possible.

It is certainly hard to believe that this scrupulous care of words,
of accent, of meaning, and of mood combined with a great
technical skill and an undoubted musical sense merely resulted
in an irreligious adaptation of secular tricks. Is it not rather
a triumph in the face of great difficulty and a religious music
which constantly approaches and often reaches true greatness?

3

Dramatic Music

WHEN at last the theatres of London were reopened after their enforced silence during the Commonwealth, Fletcher and Jonson, rattling farces, Shakespeare ' improv'd ' for the stage and heroic rants were tumbled out for the inattentive amusement of the smart courtiers and city madams. Actors no longer in danger of a whipping or imprisonment found the court open-armed to receive them, and the court in exchange found the new race of actresses no less open-hearted for them. There was but little seriousness to be discovered in the new drama that was springing up : the tragedy was fantastic and the farce preposterous—indeed the only facet of the theatre that reflected anything but an unreal world was comedy. This general atmosphere of unreality encouraged the inattention of the audience which had brought it into being, and it is not surprising that as the years went on more and more popularity was won by the spectacular inconsequent strings of clever turns that were hotch-potched together and dubbed opera.[1] This tendency was not new : the masque introduced by Shakespeare into *The Tempest* is quite as unnecessary as that in Dryden's version of the same play. Music, of course, had always been a recognized factor in the theatre, sometimes confined to a flourish or a tune on the recorders, sometimes taking the form of extraneous comic songs and dances between the scenes, and constantly used before the play began.

In 1680 [2] the play of *Theodosius* was produced at the Duke's Theatre. ' All the Parts in't being perfectly perform'd, with

[1] ' They do not matter tho' it be a Hodch Potch, for they say, they mind only the Parts as they come on one after another, and have no regard to the whole Composition ' (Sorbière, *A Voyage to England* [1663]).

[2] For the chronology of Purcell's Dramatic Music see the invaluable monograph by Mr. Barclay Squire in the *Sammelbände*.

Amphitheatra *ſile, et Spectacula Barbara Cæſar;*
Non coeunt Nudi, non Aper, Urſa, Leo.
Nos Mites colimus Muſas, lenivit Amorq;
Prælia ; cum noſtro eſt Incola Marte Venus.
Quoſq; ferunt olim Thalamo cepiſſe Theatro
Ludentes unâ cernat Apollo Deos.

III. The Duke's Theatre, Dorset Garden. From *The Empress of Morocco*,
by Elkanah Settle, 1673.

several Entertainments of Singing ; Compos'd by the Famous Master Mr. *Henry Purcell* (being the first he e'er Compos'd for the Stage) made it a living and Gainful Play to the Company.' [1] This popular drama of innocence and insipid heroics contains one long musical scene and a few songs. The music to the ritual scene [2] is simple, as would be expected from a composer of twenty in his first dramatic experiment. But the careful accentuation of the words is significant, and the dramatic effect made by the sudden silences in the preparation solo and chorus by no means negligible. The songs were in all probability sung between the acts in place of the instrumental interludes—Act Tunes as they were called—and have not the least bearing on the action, except that a song of Cupid and the weapons of the God of War precedes a love-scene between the Empress Pulcheria and Marcian, a gallant soldier.

Political unrest damned the next two plays with which Purcell was concerned, but the pathetic song in Tate's *Richard II* (1681) and the academic nauticalism of the storm song in D'Urfey's *Sir Barnaby Whigg* (1681) are not notable enough to cause any regret. Nor is Purcell's early instrumental music for the theatre of any great value : it is full of unsatisfactory rhythmic experiments, and has nothing to do with the mood of the play to which it is supposed to have been written— Fletcher's *The Double Marriage* (1688).[3] The short catch, ' My Wife has a Tongue ', may have been sung in *The English Lawyer* (1683-4 ?) by Ravenscroft ; the most brilliant sacrifice scene in *Circe* (1690) [4] may conceivably be by some other composer ; the clever military catch in *The Knight of Malta* (1686-91 ?) may never have been sung on the stage, and the

[1] Downes, *Roscius Anglicanus*.   [2] See p. 16 seq.

[3] See Allardyce Nicoll's *Restoration Drama*, p. 313.

[4] Sir George Etherege in a letter to the Duke of Buckingham, according to the *Biographia Dramatica*.

miscalled Mad Song from *Sophonisba* (1685–93 ?) is completely negligible. But the short songs in the 'monstrous and insipid'[1] *A Fool's Preferment* (1688), which was 'so solemnly interred to the tune of catcalls',[1] in spite of the well-drawn figures of farce, Cocklebrain, Grub, and Toby, deserve more than a passing notice.

All the songs but one are for Lyonel, a poor young man of the time of Henry IV, 'crown'd with Flowers, and Antickly drest', who is mad for love of Celia, a maid of honour. The first mad effusion is distorted in rhythm to give an impression of vague inconsequence, but the second, 'There's nothing so fatal as woman', is a delightful example of Purcell's triple time tunes which is full of light fancy.

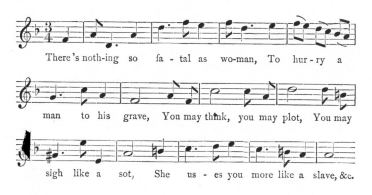

There's noth-ing so fa - tal as wo-man, To hur - ry a man to his grave, You may think, you may plot, You may sigh like a sot, She us - es you more like a slave, &c.

Lyonel next interrupts Aurelia, who is busy 'Bubling her Husband', with two dramatic fragments, 'Fled is my Love' and ''Tis Death alone', which almost show that Purcell could not resist feeling sympathy even for the madness that D'Urfey invented for laughter. The fool who hopes for preferment through his wife is interrupted in his researches

------

[1] See p. 64, note 4.

into the lore of heraldry by a heroic outburst from the mad lover :

> I'll mount to yon blue Coelum,
> To shun those female gipsies,
> I'll play at bowls with Sun and Moon,
> And scare you with Eclipses.

This extraordinary announcement was perhaps followed by the well-known mad song, ' I'll sail upon the Dog-star ': it is a bold, vigorous composition, which admirably suits Lyonel's valiant mood. At the end of the play the lover calms down and assumes folk-dance ingenuousness for his final song, ' If thou wilt give me back my love '. The only sane song is the charming pastoral dialogue, ' Jenny, 'gin you can love ', which was most likely introduced in Act IV. This forerunner of Purcell's numerous shepherd and nymph scenes with its Scottish flavour is a reflection of the growing tendency of the day to affect rural pleasures, a tendency that was admired by Herrick, Marvell, and Milton, and laughed at by D'Urfey and the town wits.

In these early years Purcell seldom wrote a song or scene that achieves a really great effect—the chorus, ' Great Minister of Fate ', from *Circe* (1690),[1] alone approaches the sublime— and his light songs and airs are often marred by an awkward rhythm : his instrumental music is very tentative, and for the most part unvaried, but his accompaniments are always interesting, and not mere supporting consonances ; but above all his experiments and his fearless attempts to test all methods of musical treatment prove his ability and foreshadow the higher levels of musical achievement that he was to reach.

The first dramatic work of any importance by Purcell was practically a challenge to the musical foreigners who were praised by a certain section with Dryden at their head at the expense of native talent. When he was asked by the dancing

---

[1] *v. supra.*

schoolmaster, Mr. Josias Priest, to write a work for the young gentlewomen of his school in Chelsea, Purcell at once seized the opportunity to show what a British composer could do in dramatic music and succeeded in producing an opera which is far more effective than *Albion and Albanius* (1685)—the work by his French rival Grabu, so belauded by Dryden—but which is so full of sympathy for human weakness, so tinged with an understanding kindness, and yet so technically well made that it was too advanced for its time, and was fated to be isolated in its brilliance.

This opera was the famous *Dido and Aeneas* (1688–9?), written by Purcell in his thirtieth year to a doggerel libretto by the Poet Laureate, Nahum Tate.

Briefly, the story is this. Dido, filled with a melancholy love for her guest, the Prince Aeneas, escorts him to hunt in the hills near the town. Suddenly a storm brewed by some anarchistic witches springs up and the court is frightened back to Carthage, leaving Aeneas to be accosted by a sorceress, who, in the guise of Mercury, orders him to set sail at once for the shores of Italy. The pious prince bids farewell to Dido, his ships put out, and the forsaken queen dies in the arms of her maidens.

The mood of the opera is set by the first section of the overture with its poignant falling discords and the glorious air in which the queen replies to her consoling confidante. This marvellous solo, which with its heavy sighs recalls Venus's lament at the death of Adonis in Dr. Blow's masque-opera, *Venus and Adonis* (1685), would seem unsurpassable if it were not known that the famous death song is to follow : the pathetic fragility of the sighs, the tragedy conveyed by the low register of the voice on the word ' torment ', the pent-up grief of the lament, ' I languish till my grief is known ', the heart-rending cry, ' Yet would not have it guessed ', and the

Peace and I are stran-gers, stran-gers grown.

(Fig. bass.)

Strings.

&c.

overwhelming effect of the entry of the strings on the last note of the voice-part, combine to make this one of the most wonderful songs that Purcell ever wrote. The rest of the first scene is bright and tuneful, and ends with a chorus of experimental form and a vigorous *Triumphing Dance*.

When the scene changes to a gloomy cave where the sorceress and the witches hatch their plots, there is a strange foreboding prelude that is perhaps the most successful of all Purcell's descriptive music hitherto—the amazing effect of uncanny darkness conveyed by the sudden change from F minor to the dominant seventh in G minor is particularly remarkable. After a sinister exhortation by the sorceress (a bass part), which is apparently a deliberate copy of a similar passage in *Albion*

and *Albanius* (Act II), the witches burst out in a striking
chorus, 'Harm's our delight'. This with the awkward and
ungainly changes, which give a clever impression of the weird
beldames and their queer, grotesque actions, is a successful
attempt at description such as the French musician never
could have imagined. The witches cackle with laughter at
the plan of their agitator, conjure up a storm on hearing the
hunt in the distance, and dance an unholy Pyrrhic dance to
the accompaniment of *Thunder and lightning, horrid music.*
The Furies sink down in the cave, the rest fly up.[1] The second
act ends with the hunting scene in a grove near the town,
which is interrupted by the stormburst which sends the
courtiers scurrying for shelter. Aeneas sadly promises to obey
the commands of the false Mercury, and the witches express
their joy at their success in 'The Groves Dance'.[2]

Act III. *Scene the Ships. Enter the Saylors. The Sorceress
and her Inchanteresses.* A vigorous triple time prelude intro-
duces the sailor's song, 'Come away, fellow sailors, come
away'. This is a model for a stage chanty, and would have
been far more acceptable to the 'blunt Tarpawlin' in *Sir
Barnaby Whigg* (1681) than the concert-room sea-piece with
which Purcell regaled him. The chorus of sailors and their

---

[1] All the words and stage directions are quoted from the printed libretto.
[2] The music to this is lost.

sweethearts is swept off its feet by the lilt of the refrain, and all join in a characteristic dance that is full of happy-go-lucky high spirits, and clearly invites clumping villagers to jig round together. The witches, rejoicing that

> our plot has took,
> the queen's forsook,

give vent to their creed at the thought of the coming wreck of Aeneas in a simple but effective chorus which must have been written expressly for amateur performers :

> Destruction's our delight,
>   Delight's our greatest sorrow !
> Elissa bleeds tonight,
>   And Carthage flames tomorrow.

This scene closes with a Jack-a-lantern dance to display the ingenuity of Mr. Priest and his dancing pupils. Aeneas, torn between love and duty, hurries away, and Dido, broken by his faithlessness and heedless of the praises of the chorus, sinks down and slowly, sadly dies.

> Thy hand, Belinda ; darkness shades me :
>   On thy bosom let me rest :
> More I would, but Death invades me :
>   Death is now a welcome guest.
> When I am laid in earth, may my wrongs create
>   No trouble in thy breast ;
> Remember me, but ah ! forget my fate.

So with these poor words that cannot be made to scan, and with some of the most poignant music that has ever been written, while ' Cupids appear in the Clouds o're her Tomb ', Dido, Queen of Carthage, dies, and weeping cupids scatter roses on her tomb, while the chorus softly leave the Loves to guard her.

It is amazing how much value is packed into this little work, which lasts barely an hour. The preludes to each act, the melancholy despair of the queen, the unholy glee and warped minds of the witches, the distant hunt, the sudden storm, the fresh-air cleanliness of the sailors' scene, the touches of realism in the recitatives, the quiet pathos of the last scene, and the numberless and varied dances are all remarkable achievements, quite apart from the many proofs of technical skill with which the opera is full. It is impossible to admire any part at the expense of another : Dido's death-song is a marvellous piece of dramatic writing ; it is supremely beautiful as music, and is technically as remarkable an achievement as the queen's first song, which is also written on a ground ; yet Purcell is no less successful in the eleven dances which were naturally included for Mr. Priest's delectation : pantomimic, comic, stately, bucolic, weird, charming—all are composed with astounding knowledge of the stage, which perhaps was not so much knowledge as instinct. In technique, invention, and sense of dramatic effect, Purcell is supreme, but, as Parry says in the *Oxford History of Music*, it is the sincerity of *Dido and Aeneas* that makes it such a superb work as a whole.

In 1690 Purcell was again working with Priest, this time in a spectacular version of Beaumont and Fletcher's *The Prophetess*, by the great actor, Thomas Betterton. This so-called opera was produced at the Dorset Garden Theatre, which was well equipped with stage machinery, and ' being set out with costly scenes, machines, and clothes, . . . it gratified the expectation of Court and City, and got the author great reputation '.[1] In the following year, Purcell published the score—a rare event in those days, but in this case most likely urged by the fact that Grabu had printed his music to *Albion and Albanius*. This publication, like the production itself, resulted in a financial loss, but the music brought Purcell into touch with Dryden, and gave him great reputation as a dramatic composer.

[1] Downes.

The music to *Dioclesian*—as Purcell himself called this opera—is very considerable. After the conventional First and Second Music—which ' diverts your time till the Play begins, and the People chuse to go in betimes to hear it ' [1]— the overture and the First Act Tune, there is a huge musical scene of triumph with solos and choruses in which ' All sing great Diocles' story ', *While they invest him with the Imperial Robes.* Dioclesian, rewarded with the hand of Aurelia for avenging the Emperor's death, momentarily forgets his betrothed Drusilla, but is soon reminded of his delinquency when

> ' *The stage is darkened on a sudden. A dreadful Monster comes from the farther end of the Scenes, and moves slowly forward . . . The Musick flourish. They who made the Monster separate in an instant and fall into a Figure, ready to begin a Dance of Furies.*'

The careful characterization of each section of this long dance points inevitably to the fact that Purcell, inspired no doubt by Priest, was greatly interested in stage dancing, and well understood both what was suitable music for dancing and also what contrasts were effective on the stage.

After a beautiful prelude for two flutes—a canon two in one on a ground—there is an amusing dance of ' Cane Chairs ' which entertained the gallery,[2] and which is closely followed by the famous song, ' What shall I do to show how much I love her '. A skilfully impressionistic ' Dance of Butterflies ' occurs in the next scene, and the fourth act ends with another musical triumph in which the chorus rather nonchalantly take up the song—

[1] Sorbière, on the ' Learning, Religion, And other Curiosities ' of England in *A Voyage to England* [in 1663], London, 1709. This preliminary concert had been practised since the old Blackfriars Theatre days.

[2] See the prologue to *The Fairy Queen.*

Let all rehearse
In lofty verse
Great Dioclesian's glory.

At last, in the final act, there is a long masque with music that well repays the comparative tedium of the earlier musical scenes—a tedium that is relieved by an occasional song or dance, and that is only real when Purcell's full powers are considered. Cupid calls on all the rustic deities, the Graces and Pleasures, Bacchanalians and Silvans, to join in universal revelry. Dioclesian and the presumably Roman soldiers are edified by this display on the part of the good sorceress, Delphia. But she is not content with such a poor exhibition, and she exerts her utmost powers.

'While a Symphony is Playing, a Machine descends, so large, it fills all the Space, from the Frontispiece of the Stage, to the farther end of the House; and fixes it self by two Ladders of Clouds to the Floor. In it are Four several Stages, representing the Pallaces of two Gods, and two Goddesses: The first is the Pallace of *Flora*; the Columns of red and white Marble, breaking through the Clouds; the Columns Fluted and Wreath'd about with all sorts of Flow'rage; the Pedestals and Flutings inrich'd with Gold. The Second is, The Pallace of the Goddess *Pomona*, the Columns of blue Marble, wound about with all kind of Fruitage, and inrich'd with Gold as the other. The Third is, The Pallace of *Bacchus*, the Columns of green Marble, Wreath'd and Inrich'd with Gold, with Clusters of Grapes hanging round 'em. The last is the Pallace of the Sun; it is supported on either Side by Rows of *Termes*, the lower part white Marble, the upper part Gold. The whole Object is terminated with a glowing Cloud, on which is a Chair of State, all of Gold, the Sun breaking through the Cloud, and making a Glory about it: As this descends, there rises from under the Stage a pleasant Prospect of a Noble Garden, consisting of Fountains, and Orange Trees set in large Vases: the middle Walk leads to a Pallace at

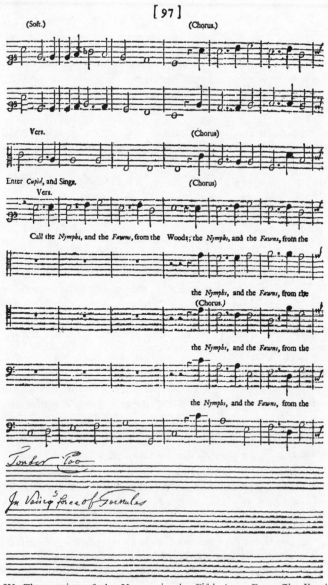

IV. The opening of the Masque in the Fifth Act. From *The Vocal and Instrumental Musick of the Prophetess, or the History of Dioclesian.* J. Heptinstall, for the Author: London, 1691.

a great distance. At the same time Enters *Silvanus, Bacchus, Flora, Pomona*, Gods of the Rivers, *Fawns, Nymphs, Hero's, Heroines, Shepherds, Shepherdesses*, the *Graces*, and *Pleasures*, with all the rest of their followers. The Dancers place themselves on every Stage in the Machine : the Singers range themselves about the Stage.'

The whole of the musical setting to this amazing scene, with the exception of the ineffective experiment in counter-rhythms, ' Let monarchs fight ', is admirable. The opening chorus to Cupid, the trumpet ' Paspe ', the rondo for the two soprano Wood-Gods, the comic Bacchic duet ' Make room ', the Bacchanal dance, the delicate song ' Still I'm wishing, still desiring ', the tripping dance ' Canaries ', the charming pastoral duet, the country dance, the splendid chorus ' Begone, begone, importunate reason ', the rustic dance with its five-bar rhythm, and the final superb chorus, ' Triumph, victorious Love ', make a musical scene that is every whit as amazing as the stage presentation. This brief catalogue can do little to show the magnificence of the music, and no verbal description can give any idea of the power of the music to this masque.

Purcell here, for the first time, was providing music for what was at the time called ' opera '. *Dido and Aeneas* was a freak, and though he may have caught from it a glimpse of what might be possible in the way of dramatic music, and would have welcomed the opportunity to try his hand at a realistic opera of human emotions, Purcell was forced to comply with the accepted idea described by Dryden in the preface to *Albion and Albanius*.

' An *Opera* is a poetical Tale or Fiction, represented by Vocal and Instrumental Musick, adorn'd with Scenes, Machines and Dancing. The suppos'd Persons of this musical Drama, are generally supernatural, as Gods and Goddesses, and Heroes, which at least are descended from them, and are in due time, to be adopted into their Number.

The Subject therefore being extended beyond the Limits of Humane Nature, admits of that sort of marvellous and surprizing conduct, which is rejected in other Plays.'

Here there are enough ' Scenes, Machines and Dancing ' in all conscience, and the conduct is surely sufficiently ' marvellous and surprizing ' to justify the title of ' opera ' in the Dryden sense.

Confined in this way to extraordinary scenes, Purcell naturally spent his energies in developing the range of his musical power. He had already seen the necessity for some system of tonality, and took great care that all the long musical scenes should be bound together by a key. In *Dido and Aeneas* the instrumental parts had been necessarily simple, but here he shows the greatest care to provide accompaniments that are not only interesting in themselves, but also to each player. He is constantly grasping every opportunity to obtain contrast, and is always trying new ' colour ' effects. Hampered as he must have been in his first important work for the theatre, he occupied his energies in improving his powers, not only as a composer, but especially as a dramatic composer, in the hope that when the chance came for him to have a free hand he might apply the technical knowledge he had acquired and produce at last an English opera that would at least be superior to a foreign import.

Dryden was undoubtedly the dramatist from whom such a chance might come, and he was won over to Purcell by his music for *Dioclesian*. The wary poet immediately tested the composer's powers by inviting him to provide the music for his new comedy, *Amphitryon* (1690). Purcell justified the commission, as Dryden unexpectedly admits in the dedicatory letter that was printed with the play :

' But what has been wanting on my Part, has been abundantly supplyed by the Excellent Composition of Mr

Purcell ; in whose Person we have at length found an *English-Man,* equal with the best abroad. At least my Opinion of him has been such, since his happy and judicious Performances in the late *Opera* ; and the Experience I have had of him, in the setting my three Songs for this *Amphitryon.* To all which, and particularly to the Composition of the *Pastoral Dialogue,* the numerous Quire of Fair Ladies gave so just an Applause on the Third Day.'

Purcell's contribution to the play, which with the music to *Dioclesian* caused Dryden's sudden *volte-face,* consisted of an overture, seven other instrumental numbers, two songs, and the long pastoral dialogue. There is nothing remarkably striking about this music. It is all very delightful and humorous and admirably suitable to the farcical comedy, but there is nothing much more than tunefulness and charm except in the dialogue, which is a real advance on the two earlier experiments in this form. But it is vastly important in the history of Purcell's dramatic music, for it was the trial work for Dryden, and resulted in close collaboration with the leading poet and dramatist of the day.

Purcell was concerned with three other plays before his great chance came and he was asked to collaborate with Dryden in the production of his great patriotic work, *King Arthur* (1691). The playwright actually went so far as to modify his words for the sake of the music, if we are to take Dryden's words sincerely.

' There is nothing better, than what I intended, but the Musick ; which has since arriv'd to a greater Perfection in *England,* than ever formerly especially passing through the Artful Hands of Mr *Purcel,* who has Compos'd it with so great a Genius, that he has nothing to fear but an ignorant, ill-judging Audience. But the Numbers of Poetry and Vocal Musick, are sometimes so contrary, that in many places I have been oblig'd to cramp my Verses, and make them rugged to the Reader, that they may be harmonious to the Hearer : Of which I have no Reason to repent me, because these sorts of Entertainment are principally design'd for the Ear and Eye ; and therefore in Reason my Art on this occasion, ought to be subservient to his. And besides, I flatter my self with an Imagination, that a Judicious Audience will easily distinguish betwixt the Songs, wherein I have comply'd with him, and those in which I have followed the Rules of Poetry, in the Sound and Cadence of the Words.' [1]

The last sentence would seem to imply that Dryden did not accept Purcell's suggestion with too good a grace, but that, feeling bound to adopt the advice of a popular favourite, he trusted the intelligent audience to discriminate. The audience, in all probability, paid much more attention to the music and machines than to the spoken dialogue, and listened to the sound of the songs rather than to the words that were being sung, either because they were not as intelligent as Dryden pretended, or because they preferred not to have to think of the rules of poetry.

King Arthur is completely negligible as a play by Dryden and curiously uneven as an opera by Purcell. The chief incidents concern the rival spirits Philidel and Grimbald, the servants of Merlin and Osmond, and the magic that is practised by both sides allows for several interludes and masques. But the fundamental plot turns on the rivalry between Oswald, the heathen Saxon king of Kent, and Arthur for love of Emmeline, the blind heiress of the Duke of Cornwall. She is captured by Oswald, who will not release her. Osmond, an evil magician, makes love to her rather in the manner of Monostatos in *The Magic Flute*, but having regained her sight through Merlin's charms, she spurns him and is rescued by Arthur, who, after many adventures, makes peace with Oswald as an excuse for introducing a magnificent masque to dazzle the audience.

---

[1] Epistle Dedicatory to *King Arthur*.

The first act contains a scene of heathen sacrifice by the Saxons, a battle and the triumph-song of the Britons, ' Come, if you dare '. The difference between this British song of victory and the choruses of the heathen Saxons is remarkable, for the former is clear-cut, melodious, and full of rhythm, while the enemy's music, though beautiful in its own way and not in the least suitable (according to our present ideas) to the fierce and evil natures of the foes by whom it is sung, is contrapuntal and intricate. It is very tempting, in view of the 'Handelian' style of the Saxon choruses, to imagine that Purcell was here indulging in a slight musical parody and was imitating perhaps Buxtehude or Pachelbel in the Saxon music, while for the British refrains he relied on the honest directness of the folk-songs of his native country.

The second act is relieved by two of the most charming scenes that Purcell ever wrote. The first is the rival wooing of the king by good and evil spirits. Philidel, disguised as a shepherd, is intent on saving Arthur from the clutches of the ' earthy spirit ' Grimbald, who is equally intent to lead him into the ' trembling bogs, that bear a green-sward show '. The good spirits triumph, Grimbald ' sinks with a flash ', and the Britons are led safely past the morass to the strains of Philidel's attendants, ' Come follow, follow, follow me '. It would be inadequate to attempt to quote from this delightful music. There is no attempt to distinguish between the good and bad spirits, for all were in the guise of kindly shepherds, but the antiphonal singing gives the atmosphere as clearly as if the varied dispositions were accurately characterized.

The other is a pastoral entertainment that is most unsuitably acted for Emmeline, who, being blind, can hardly have enjoyed the dancing, though she may have revelled in the music. ' How blest are shepherds ' is certainly one of the most tuneful songs of the seventeenth century: the melody is smooth and flowing, and the charming modulations lead gently up to the climax and then quietly fall to a peaceful ending.

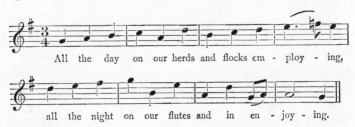

While the hautboys play a prelude, ' the men offer their flutes to the women, which they refuse ': two shepherdesses then sing the dainty ' Shepherds, shepherds, leave decoying ', and demand their signatures to marriage-vows. The men comply, and all join in a jovial chorus, ' Come, shepherds, lead up a lively measure '. The scene ends with a hornpipe for the rustics and a clash of wills and arms between Arthur and his rival Oswald.

The ' Frost Scene ', which has so often been quoted as Purcell's greatest achievement in dramatic music, is created by Osmond's magic to prove to Emmeline the supreme power of love. The ' Scene changes to a prospect of Winter in frozen countries ', and the ' Genius of the Clime ', summoned by Cupid, sings the wonderful song which has given the whole scene the touch of genius. The chromatic rise and fall of the melody, the soft reiteration of the strings and the occasional tremolando marks in the vocal part—copied from a similar scene in Lulli's *Isis*—give to this song the pathetic, cold realism on which the scene depends and which is supremely moving. But the rest of the representation of the thawing of numbed fingers by the power of love is poor by comparison with the other musical scenes with which the operas are filled.

The final masque called up by Merlin for the delectation of the newly allied Britons and Saxons is a magnificent display of the homage given to the ' Queen of Islands ' by all the sea-creatures. This long musical scene includes a charming duet for Pan and a Nereid, the remarkable trio ' For folded flocks ', and the marvellous song ' that time has not the power to injure. It is of all ages and countries '.[1] The words of this song, ' Fairest Isle, all Isles excelling ', are reminiscent of the wonderful poem that Catallus wrote on the gem of all islands and sea-washed tongues of land, Sirmio, and the melody is perhaps the most beautiful of all Purcell's unpassionate and non-characterized songs. It is, indeed, one of those melodies that by their sheer loveliness cloud the beauties of all music that is played after them. Here the duet, trumpet-song, chorus, and dance that follow are barely good of their kind, and the drop is even more noticeable. *King Arthur*, indeed, like this concluding masque, is a most uneven work. It certainly contains some of Purcell's best music, but it also has more tedious moments than any other of his dramatic compositions. Dr. Arne, indeed, goes so far as to think that some of the solos in this opera ' are infamously bad—so very bad, that they are privately the objects of sneer and ridicule to the Musicians ';[2] but this was written in a prejudiced letter to Garrick when Arne was hoping to be employed to write all the music for the forthcoming revival of the opera. Half the music in this work is undeniably excellent, but the other half is infinitely more lengthy, and as a whole *Dioclesian* is distinctly the better work. But when all is said, ' Fairest Isle ' or the pastoral scene more than balances the flatness of ' Saint George '.[3]

In 1691 Purcell provided a small amount of instrumental

[1] Burney, iii. 492.

[2] From a letter to Garrick quoted in a catalogue of Messrs. Maggs.

[3] I have been unable to find any copy of this song earlier than the nineteenth-century version published by the Musical Antiquarian Society.

music for four unimportant plays, and in the following year was again associated with Priest in

> ' a New Opera, wherein something very surprising is promised us ' [1] . . . ' it is call'd *The Fairy Queen.* The *Drama* is originally *Shakespears,* the *Music* and *Decorations* are extraordinary. I have heard the Dances commended, and without doubt the whole is very entertaining.' [2]

Downes was no less enthusiastic than Motteux :

> ' This in Ornaments was Superior to the other Two ; ' (*Dioclesian* and *King Arthur*) ' especially in Cloaths, for all the Singers and Dancers, Scenes, Machines and Decorations, all most profusely set off ; and excellently perform'd, chiefly the Instrumental and Vocal part Compos'd by the said Mr *Purcel,* and Dances by Mr *Priest.* The Court and Town were wonderfully satisfy'd with it ; but the Expences in setting it out being so great, the Company got very little by it.'

So expensive was the whole production that the speaker of the Prologue made a special appeal :

> *But that this Play may in its Pomp appear ;*
> *Pray let our Stage from thronging Beaux be clear.*
> *For what e're cost we're at, what e're we do,*
> *In Scenes, Dress, Dances ; yet there 's many a Beau,*
> *Will think himself a much more taking Show.*
> *How often have you curs'd these new* Beau-skreens,
> *That stand betwixt the Audience and the Scenes ?*

> *I ask'd one of 'em t'other day*—Pray, Sir,
> Why d'ye the Stage before the Box prefer ?
> *He answer'd*—O ! there I Ogle the whole Theatre,
> My Wig—my Shape, my Leg, I there display,
> They speak much finer things than I can say.

This masking of the stage by beaux from the audience must have been a real fear to the producer of *The Fairy Queen,* who

---

[1] *Gentleman's Journal* for January 1692.　　　[2] Ibid. for May 1692.

was in a strong position to disprove the strictures of Richard
Flecknoe on the subject of those ' excellent helps of imagination, most grateful deceptions of the sight, and graceful and
becoming Ornaments of the Stage ', scenes and machines. He
had accused the English of being

> ' only Schollars and Learners yet, having proceeded no
> further than to bare painting, and not arriv'd to the stupen-
> dous wonders of your great Ingeniers, especially not knowing
> yet how to place our Lights, for the more advantage and
> illuminating of the Scenes.' [1]

By the time *The Fairy Queen* was ready for production the
technique of stage machinery in England must have been
exceedingly advanced—no doubt under Betterton's direction,
for he had been to France to study the question there [2]—and
the difficult question of lighting well understood, for, magnificent though the scenic descriptions are in *Dioclesian* and
King Arthur, they are utterly beggared by the stupendous
directions in *The Fairy Queen*, which may seem to present-day
readers most out of place, but must certainly astonish with
their splendour even those who are familiar with the mechanical
devices of the modern theatre.

This magnificent ' opera ' is, in fact, a glorious revue hotch-
potch grafted or rather jammed on to an ' improved ' version
of *A Midsummer-Night's Dream*. Never did Purcell so consistently write delightful music. It is almost pointless to mention the individual numbers, so perfect is each. Here there

---

[1] *A Discourse of the English Stage*, 16 (?).

[2] 1683, Sept. 22. Lord Preston to Duke of York: ' Mr. Betterton
coming hither some weeks since by his Majesty's command, to endeavour
to carry over the Opera, and finding that impracticable, did treat with
Monsr. Grahme [Grabu ?] to go over with him to endeavour to represent
something at least like an opera in England for his Maiesty's diversion '
(Hist. MSS. Comm., 7th Report, Part I, p. 290).

is no average level of merit, all is of the highest possible calibre. *The Fairy Queen* is without question Purcell's masterpiece.

It may be a matter of regret that Shakespeare's poetry was butchered with unnecessary or inapposite interpolations, but the masques with which the opera is sprinkled all containgems of music, and are in their entirety brilliant conceptions by a genius. It is hard to avoid being fulsome. Dismissing the First and Second Music and the grand Overture, the first music to be noticed is the delicious scene of the Fairies and the Drunken Poet.

DRUNKEN POET.

Fi - fi - fi - fi!l up the bowl, then fi - fi - fi - fill up the bowl, then fi - fi - fi - fill up the bowl, then

FIRST FAIRY.

Trip it, trip it, trip it, trip it, trip it, trip it in a ring : a -

&c.

The thistle-down lightness of the mischievous sprites and the coarse hiccoughs of their poor victim are reproduced equally well, and for character and humour this scene would be hard

to rival. Long Fairy revels accompanied by the voices of all the
' songsters of the sky ',

with distant echoes sounding through the woods, at length tire
Titania, and she is visited by Night, Secrecy, Mystery, and
Sleep, who, in a quiet lullaby that hardly dares to break the
deep silence of the woods, close those eyes on which Oberon
drops the magic ' love-juice '.

The usual pastoral scene is introduced into the third act, but it is a pastoral scene that is lengthened and magnified beyond all recognition, just as Bottom, for whom it is performed, is translated. 'If Love's a sweet passion', 'Ye gentle spirits of the air',[1] the delicious Coridon and Mopsa duet, the tuneful 'When I have often heard', are the chief vocal numbers, and are balanced by an Entry of two Swans, a Fairies' Dance, 'The Dance for the Green Men', and a Dance for the Haymakers.' Words must fail to convey the least impression of what is thoroughly charming. The music of the whole of this masque is exquisite, and in performance the effect is overwhelming.

After the reconciliation of the Fairy King and Queen

'*the Sun rises, it appears red through the Mist, as it ascends it dissipates the Vapours, and is seen in its full Lustre ; then the Scene is perfectly discovered, the Fountains enrich'd with gilding, and adorn'd with Statues : The view is terminated by a Walk of Cypress Trees which lead to a delightful Bower. Before the Trees stand rows of Marble Columns, which support many Walks which rise by Stairs to the top of the House ; the Stairs are adorn'd with Figures on Pedestals, and Rails ; and Balasters on each side of 'em. Near the top, vast Quantities of Water break out of the Hills, and fall in mighty Cascade's to the bottom of the Scene, to feed the Fountains which are on each side. In the middle of the Stage is a very large Fountain, where the Water rises about twelve Foot.*'

This glory, which precedes the appearance of Phoebus and his devoted Four Seasons, is in honour of ' the birthday of King Oberon '. The whole of this scene is as majestic as the last was charming. Each of the Seasons is brilliantly characterized, and the final superb acclamation is immense in its grandeur.

[1] This very beautiful coloratura song was added by Purcell for the revival of the opera in the following year.

From the prelude to *Winter's Song*.

It would seem that the invention of the scene-and-machine designer had been already exploited to its utmost. The second act, it is true, merely was allowed a change of scene to '*a Prospect of Grotto's, Arbors, and delightful Walks*', but the third act could boast a transformation to a wood, with a river and an arch of two great dragons which vanished into thin air when the swimming swans turned into fairies, and the arrival of Phoebus in a chariot drawn by four horses in all the glory of the glistening fountains might well be thought an adequate entertainment. But, in despair of finding yet another spectacular scene, the author and producer turned their attention to a country where all was totally different to nature as it was known in Europe. Oberon and his attendants arrive in Duke Theseus's palace with '*strange Musick, warbling in the Air*'.

> You shall stranger things behold.
> Mark the wonders shall appear,
> While I feast your eye and ear.

After Juno, in a '*Machine drawn by Peacocks*' which '*spread their Tails and fill the middle of the Theatre*', has blest the reunited lovers, Oberon gives this sure proof of his supernatural powers.

> Now let a new Transparent World be seen,
> All Nature joyn to entertain our Queen.
> Now we are reconcil'd, all things agree
> To make an Universal Harmony.

' *While the Scene is darken'd a single Entry is danced ; Then a Symphony is play'd ; after that the Scene is suddainly Illuminated, and discovers a transparent Prospect of a Chinese Garden, the Architecture, the Trees, the Plants, the Fruit, the Birds, the Beasts quite different to what we have in this part of the World. It is terminated by an Arch, through which is seen other Arches with close Arbors, and a row of Trees to the end of the View. Over it is a hanging Garden, which rises by several ascents to the top of the House ; it is bounded on either side with pleasant Bowers, various Trees, and numbers of strange Birds flying in the Air, on the Top of a Platform is a Fountain, throwing up Water, which falls into a large Basin.*'

Chinese lovers appear, ' *Six Monkeys come from between the Trees, and Dance* ', the Chinese women sing songs of triumph, Hymen appears at their invocation, ' *Six Pedestals of China-work rise from under the Stage ; they support six large Vases of Porcelain, in which are six* China-Orange-Trees ', Hymen's torch bursts into flame, ' *The Pedestals move towards the Front of the Stage and the Grand Dance begins of Twenty-four Persons ; then Hymen and the Two Women sing together* ', and the amazing scene is brought to an end with a Chaconne and chorus. Musically, this masque is perhaps barely as good as the rest of the opera, but the triumph-songs, the humorous Monkeys' Dance, and the brilliant Chaconne amply make up for what hypercritics might be tempted to consider a shade inferior.

Whatever may be thought of the whole notion of tricking out *A Midsummer Night's Dream* with extraneous songs and dances, it must be admitted that Purcell's music more than makes up for the 'improvements'. It is almost impossible for the casual reader to understand the appreciation of such fantastic scenes that all audiences felt in the seventeenth century. But the wonder is, not that they saw nothing strange in holding up the action for some spectacular effect, but that Purcell's music managed to find a footing and even become popular. As the comedies of the day show, the average Londoner knew nothing of music, but merely practised it to be in the fashion : yet in all this welter of ignorant nonchalance, Purcell not only perfected his powers and so experimented that his music in all its beauty anticipated the music of future centuries, but actually became the favourite composer of the theatre-going public of his day.

After these three great works—*Dioclesian* (1690), *King Arthur* (1691), and *The Fairy Queen* (1691)—and the brilliant complete opera, *Dido and Aeneas* (1698–9), it is not necessary to give a detailed account of the rest of Purcell's dramatic music. In the remaining three years of his life he was the composer of the music for no less than thirty-one plays. Of these only four contain more than a small amount of music : *Oedipus* (1692), *Timon of Athens* (1694) with its charming masque of Cupid and Bacchus, *Bonduca* (1695), and *The Tempest* (1690?). Others contain but one or two songs, and several are merely provided with instrumental music for dances and interludes. Eight times did Dryden collaborate with Purcell in these three years—if indeed he had any hand in the operatic version of *The Tempest* as set by Purcell— D'Urfey, Southerne, and Shadwell had plays produced with his music, and it was Purcell's incidental pieces that accompanied Congreve's first dramatic essays into the world.

'The Tempest, (or) the Inchanted Island, made into an Opera by Mr. *Shadwell*,[1] having all New in it; as Scenes, Machines; particularly, one Scene Painted with Myriads of *Ariel* Spirits . . . not any succeeding Opera got more Money.'[2]

This extraordinary perversion of Shakespeare's play—more extraordinary with its double set of characters than *The Fairy Queen*—'is one of the . . . best of Purcell's Compositions for the Stage'.[3] It contains the two graceful songs for Ariel, 'Come unto these yellow sands' and 'Full fathom five', with the subtle impressions of the clash of distant muffled bells, a charming song, 'Dear pretty youth', which occurs in a scene which alone of the pathetic moments in Restoration plays succeeds in its pathos—the scene in which Dorinda tries to wake the dead Hippolito—a short masque of devils, the magnificent masque called up by Prospero.

'Neptune, Amphitrite, Oceanus, *and* Tethys, *appear in Chariot drawn with Sea-horses; on each side of the Chariot Sea-Gods, and Goddesses, Tritons, and Nereids*.'

These 'amazing objects', as Antonio calls them, are accompanied by vigorous music that is tinged with the very breath of the sea from which the deities come. Even if the airs 'Halcyon Days', 'See the heavens smile', and the scene 'Aeolus, you must appear', were not notable for their musical value—and they are all conceived with an unsullied grandeur that Purcell seldom attempted—this masque would be remarkable for containing what is perhaps the earliest example of leitmotiv, for a characteristic phrase representing the quiet play of ripples on the surface of the ocean is twice used in different places.

[1] The whole bibliography of the operatic *Tempest* needs careful examination. There are versions by Dryden-Davenant and Shadwell, and the version set by Purcell is different again.

[2] Downes, *Roscius Anglicanus*.   [3] Ibid.

From *See, see the heavens smile.*

From *Aeolus, you must appear.*

Though *The Tempest* is the only opera among the later dramatic music in which a consistently high level is kept, almost every play with which Purcell was connected contains some song or dance which is at least as good as any in *Dioclesian* or *The Fairy Queen*. His treatment of the pastoral scene, which has been so often mentioned in the course of this chapter, perhaps reached perfection in *The Libertine* (1692–5 ?)—Shadwell's strange version of *Don Juan*. The shepherds and shepherdesses, who merely provide an incident in the shameless career of Don John, the 'rash, fearless Man, guilty of all Vice', hold up the action unnecessarily with their conscious simplicity, but the rightly famed 'Nymphs and Shepherds' and the following chorus, 'We come, we come', which turns into the equally well-known 'In these delightful pleasant groves', are well worth the temporary shattering of the dramatic interest—which is indeed never any stronger than mere melodrama.

The sacrifice scenes—first essayed by Purcell in *Theodosius* (1680) and *Circe* (1690)—are splendidly employed in *The*

Libertine (1692–5 ?), *The Indian Queen* (1695), *Bonduca* (1695), and the queer melodramatization of *Oedipus* by Dryden and Lee (1692). In the Sophocles-Dryden play, Purcell has also added a touch of the witches from *Dido and Aeneas* (1688–9)— a mood that is admirably in keeping with the ' *Peal of Thunder : and Flashes of Lightning : then Groaning beneath the Stage* ' which herald the arrival of the ghosts that ' justle one another in the dark '.[1] The mad songs in *A Fool's Preferment* (1688) find an echo in *The Richmond Heiress* (1693) and *Tyrannic Love* (1694–5). The success of the ' Frost Scene ' invocation and the song of Winter in *The Fairy Queen* (1691) is repeated in the magnificent Ismeron-Zempoalla scene in *The Indian Queen* (1695), in which the brilliance of Purcell's realistic touches is only equalled by the weird appearance of the God of Sleep and the last quiet bars of lulling melody.

Trumpet-songs and martial choruses again appear in *Bonduca* (1695) and *Don Quixote* (1694–5). Amorous dialogues are favourite attractions in several of the plays, and Purcell's supreme skill in portraying the pathos of grief is again shown in Bonvica's lament (*Bonduca*) and the song in *Don Quixote*, ' From rosy bowers ', ' the last Song that the Author Sett, it being in his Sickness ',[2] which is, according to Grove,

> ' one of the greatest compositions he ever produced, and the most striking proof that, however the composer's frame might be enfeebled by disease, his mental powers remained vigorous and unimpaired to the last '.

In purely instrumental music, Purcell was no less successful than in the various moods that he was called upon to illustrate in songs and choruses. His incidental music to *The Old Bachelor* (1693), *The Double Dealer* (1693), *The Married Beau* (1694), *The Rival Sisters* (1695), and especially the overtures, inter-

---

[1] Thomas Brown, ' *To George Moult Esq: from the* Gun *Musick-Booth* in *Smithfield*, Aug. 30, 1699 '.   [2] *Orpheus Britannicus.*

ludes and dances in *The Virtuous Wife* (1691 ?), and the mysterious play, *The Gordian Knot Untied* (1691), are all delightful, and deserve a better fate than to be buried as trappings to plays that perhaps were lucky enough to be honoured with a few more than three performances.

4
Odes and Welcome Songs

FROM his boyhood Purcell had been employed, like his father and uncle before him, in the service of the court. He attended Charles II at Windsor as a chorister in the Chapel Royal, which provided deans, chaplains, and choir for the use of the court wherever it might happen to be, and in 1677 he was appointed a composer in ordinary for the violin in the place of Matthew Lock, late composer to His Majesty. For the salary that was due to them the king's composers were expected to provide music for all extraordinary occasions. The royal band, or ' private musick' as it was called, which had been in existence in one form or another for hundreds of years, had recently suffered a serious change. The old ' consorts of viols' were given up in favour of the ' twenty-four violins' which the king introduced in imitation of the famous band belonging to Louis XIV, the gay host of his exile. This ' light, fantastical' innovation was by no means approved by the older members of the musical world, but Purcell was young enough to welcome the new instruments. At first he treated them as if they were viols, providing them with flowing parts that avoided any bold leaps ; but his later scores show that he was beginning to grasp the greater possibilities offered by the violins, which with their more rounded bridges afforded little risk of the accidental touching of two strings at once, and which consequently were better displayed by more vigorous passages than had ever been available on the viols—instruments which

Purcell disliked, if we can believe the story that he wrote the catch
' Of all the instruments there are ' [1] in disparagement of them.

The first work that Purcell composed for Charles II was
A Song to welcome home His Majesty from Windsor, 9 Sept.
1680. A Welcome Song—of which this is a typical example
—was a long continuous composition for orchestra, chorus
and soloists, filled with pious flattery ' To this, our mortal
deity ', whose absence from his capital is likened to autumn,
' his presence is Spring '. Charles is often represented as a lover
returning to his faithful London, who, personified as Augusta,
welcomes him with open arms : the king and his brother,
the Duke of York, are pictured as twin stars, and Britannia is
turned into a nymph charmed in the soft embraces of Charles.
Purcell managed to set some of this fulsomeness to delightful
music that well deserves to live, but is badly hampered by
the topical and cringing nature of the words. His first Welcome Song, however, is not especially remarkable for its
beauty. The tenor solo ' Music, the food of love ' contains
the germ of his rhythmic triple-time songs [2] and the duet
for two sopranos ' When the Summer, in his glory ' is charming,
but the chief interest lies with the instrumental pieces—the
overture and three delightful ritornelli—and the obvious
experiments of technique. The opening chorus of welcome
is skilfully superimposed on the second movement of the
overture, all the voice-parts except the bass being quite
new.[3] Short phrases in the tenor solo ' Your influous approach '

[1]   Of all the instruments there are,
        None with the viol can compare ;
        Mark how the strings their order keep,
        With a whet, whet, whet, and a sweep, sweep, sweep ;
        But above all it still abounds,
        With a zingle, zingle zing and a zin-zan-zounds.
[2] Cf. the contemporary ' Hail to the Mirtle shade ' from *Theodosius*.
[3] Cf. p. 48.

are echoed by the chorus—the device that Purcell later used for the scene of the invocation of Cupid to the wood-beings in *Dioclesian,* where the solo voice is apparently caught by numerous echoes in the teeming forest—but the choral writing and the two duets show little contrapuntal ability, and the block method of composition does not here seem to promise the grand, massive effect that Purcell at times achieved.

On 27 August of the following year Charles II returned to town after a four months' stay at Windsor. He dined at Hampton Court that evening and four days later was officially welcomed home by the Lord Mayor and aldermen of the city. Purcell's contribution to the general rejoicing was the Welcome Song *Swifter, Isis, swifter flow.*[1] After a short, solemn introduction there is a continuous development of style through two alto solos and a lovely bass solo accompanied by two flutes—'Land him safely on her shore': the flowing scale passages at the beginning give a clever impression of the river by which the king is arriving, but by the end of the first three songs the mood of the scales has imperceptibly changed to the joyful ringing of bells. Purcell, strange to say, has been content with this general atmosphere—which is indeed admirably suggested—and has not translated each of the vivid words into music as was his usual custom. The first half of this ode describes the arrival of the royal barge—the same barge in which, on 17 August,

> 'his majestie past by Whitehall from Windsor . . . and went on board the ship Tyger, lord Berkely commander, and bound for the Streights; and did his lordship the honour to dine with him on board.'[2]

[1] Dr. Vaughan Williams in the Purcell Society's edition assigns this ode to 12 Oct., on the King's return from Newmarket. But Charles II would hardly have travelled by barge in October, even for the experience of coming to London from Newmarket via the Thames (v. Luttrell, *passim*).

[2] Luttrell's *Diary,* et passim.

In the second half of the ode the conventional ' Welcome, dread sir, to town ' is voiced by a pleasant trio, which is reminiscent of the *Theodosius* melodies : a tenor recounts Augusta's homage : the usual flattering likeness of the king to the sun is put into the mouths of two sopranos—a lovely duet—and the whole ode is hurriedly wound up by a short chorus of praise.

The words to which Purcell had to provide music on these congratulatory occasions were by custom over-fulsome and ridiculously extravagant, and at times were merely fatuous doggerel. Perhaps the anonymous hack was responsible for the dullness of Purcell's next Welcome Song. The Duke of York—whose popularity was never very certain, especially after his seduction of his future wife—returned from Scotland, where he had been High Commissioner since 1679, on 27 May 1682 and accordingly was welcomed by a tedious ode. The opening words are :

> What, what shall be done in behalf of the man
> In whose honour the King is delighted,
> Whose conduct abroad
> Has his enemies awed
> And ev'ry proud rebel affrighted . . .?

This typical jingle did not inspire Purcell to do more than set the words adequately with an occasional obvious tune—the best of which is the delightful melody to ' All the grandeur he possesses ' which was afterwards used in the incidental music to *The Gordian Knot Untied*.

In the same year Purcell welcomed back the royal family from Newmarket (21 Oct.) where they regularly went for ' hawking, cockfighting & raceing '[1] with *The summer's absence unconcerned we bear*—an ode which is characterized by a charming pastoral movement in the overture, an alto solo,

[1] Luttrell, 8 Sept., 1681.

which is very reminiscent of the mimed song ' Oft she visits this lov'd mountain ' in *Dido and Aeneas*, and most beautiful melodic recitatives which are full of florid passages for a brilliant bass voice.

On the afternoon of 19 July 1683, Prince George of Denmark arrived at Whitehall, ' being come to make his addresses to the lady Ann, daughter to his royall highnesse ', and on 28 July they were married at St. James's by the Bishop of London. ' A long and capital production ',[1] *From hardy climes and dangerous toils of war*, was produced by Purcell for this grand occasion, and two months later he composed a still longer work congratulating the King on his deliverance from the infamous Rye House Plot. In June there had been constant council meetings to decide the wisest course of action, the militia and trained bands were called out in London for the support of law and order, and there was no time for songs of congratulation. On 2 July an address was presented to the King by the Lord Mayor and Aldermen

' in common councill assembled, congratulating his majestie and the duke of York upon the discovery of the late conspiracy, assuring him of their lives and fortunes in defence of the government in church and state '.

Similar addresses flowed in from every town and county all through July ; August was spent by the court at Windsor and at last 9 Sept., the day ' appointed by his majesties declaration as a thanksgiveing for deliverance from the late conspiracy, was observed accordingly '.[2]

[1] Burney, iii. 504.

[2] In the Purcell Society's edition this ode is stated to have been performed at the King's return to London either in June (from Windsor), 25 Sept. (from Winchester), or 20 Oct. (from Newmarket). June, as shown above, is an unlikely date : from 8 Oct. the court was in mourning for the Queen's brother, the late King of Portugal ; 9 Sept., as being the appointed day for rejoicing, is more probable than 25 Sept.

This congratulatory ode *Fly, bold Rebellion* is on a large scale. Apart from the usual string overture and four-part choruses there are five solos for alto, tenor, and bass, two trios for two sopranos and an alto, and for alto, tenor, and bass, a quintet and a grand finale that starts with a fugal septet. The whole work is excellent, especially the delicious 9/8 movement in the overture, the alto solo on a ground ' Rivers from their channels turned ', and the magnificent finale. The perpetually recurring ' sun ' simile is again used and the ' disloyal crowd ', who are called on to ' change their notes ', are likened to clouds which only serve to intensify the after-glory of the royal beams, but which must be dispelled because

> 'Tis no business of yours
> To dispute the high Pow'rs
> As if you were the government framers.

Later in the same year Purcell wrote his first odes for St. Cecilia's Day—*Laudate Ceciliam*—a short work for alto, tenor, and bass, which was possibly written for performance in the queen's Roman Catholic chapel,[1] and a setting of Christopher Fishburn's *Welcome to all the pleasures*. The Latin work is very straightforward, with pleasing formal melodies relieved by plainsong roulades and beautifully written double trills in the duet ' Dicite Virgini '. Purcell was at this time making experiments in form and rhythm, and the clean-cut form in which this work was written [2] is most successful. The other St. Cecilia Ode contains a charming string interlude, yet another solo which is reminiscent of the *Theodosius* type of melody, and an alto solo which was popular enough to be published in *Orpheus Britannicus* and—as a harpsichord piece— in *Musick's Handmaid* (1689). Yet, though well written, this ode—like so many of Purcell's works—is hampered from

---

[1] G. E. P. Arkwright in the Purcell Society's edition.

[2] AB/CDBA/EFB.

obtaining performance to-day by the words, which here are too definitely addressed to the Musical Society which performed it. Purcell himself thought highly enough of the work to consent to its publication in the following year, and the Dedication—to the Gentlemen of the Musical Society,

> ' *And particularly the* / STEWARDS / For the YEAR ensuing./*William Bridgman*, Esq.,/*Nicholas Staggins*, Doctor in *Music* ;/*Gilbert Dolben*, Esq. ; and/Mr. *Francis Forcer* '

—was signed by Henry Purcell, ' to all Lovers of Music, *A real Friend and Servant*'.

There is no need to make much comment on the ' long composition, consisting of many different airs and choruses ',[1] *From these serene and rapturous joys,* which was only too obviously written to order ' on the king's return to Whitehall after his Summer's progress ' on 25 Sept. 1685. It is the first royal ode in which the voices are accompanied by more than the harpsichord [2] and Purcell here makes the technical experiment of making a varied repetition of the chorus ' Welcome home ' in the subdominant, but the only other point of faint interest is the magnificent execution of florid passages by the bass and alto soloists.

The first ode written for James II was for his birthday, 14 Oct. 1685, after Monmouth's rebellion. The occasion was celebrated, according to Luttrell, ' with publick demonstration of joy, as ringing of bells, store of bonefires ', and the ode *Why are all the Muses mute,* though less ' tuney ' than all the preceding odes, shows considerably more mastery of melody and dramatic effect. The actual beginning is brilliant. An alto— one Mr. Turner, who sang in all the succeeding odes—quietly accompanied by the harpsichord without any introduction

---

[1] Burney, iii. 505.

[2] Except for eight bars chorus in *Welcome vicegerent* and the bass solo in *Swifter, Isis.*

asks the question ' Why, why are all the Muses mute ? ' There
is a sudden cry from the chorus ' Awake, awake ', and in reply
the strings strike up the overture.   The second movement of
this is delightful, with a constant repetition of Purcell's favourite
rhythmic ending in triple time

which he most likely evolved from his careful attention to the
correct accentuation of the many words that have, like 'glorious',
a propenultimate stress.   Two other movements demand
special notice :

The lovely instrumental rondo which was later incorporated as a Minuet in the music to *The Gordian Knot Untied*, and the excellent finale with the masterly setting of the words 'His fame shall endure till all things decay' (see p. 100).

On the morning of King James's next birthday 'his majesties four troops of guards were drawn up in Hide Park, all new clothed very finely; and the day concluded with ringing of bells, bonefires, and a ball at court'. It was on this occasion that the finest of all Purcell's royal odes, *Ye Tuneful Muses*, was performed. The whole work is magnificent. Indeed the bald method of remarking on the charming or surprising movements seems in reference to this work even more bald than usual. The fine double fugue in the overture, the chorus 'To celebrate his so much wished return'—written in the same homophonic style as the well-known 'In these delightful pleasant groves' in the contemporary opera *The Libertine*, the admirable chromatic alto solo on a ground, and the lovely soprano duet, all are full of typical Purcell beauties. Among the many experiments in the work are the employment of a popular song of the day 'Hey boys, up go we', as the bass to a cheerful song, the imitation drum bass to a martial song, and the daring literal accompaniment to the unpoetic words 'Tune all your strings', where the violins scamper backwards and forwards on their open notes. But the best of all this excellence is the wonderful Invocation to Music. This accompanied trio for two altos and a bass is the finest of all Purcell's works for more than two solo voices and well deserves to be rescued from the oblivion into which all the Welcome Songs have been necessarily thrown by the fulsome topicality and baldness of the words.

James II's birthday in 1687 was celebrated as usual with an ode by Purcell, 'but no bonefires, being so particularly commanded'. This ode, *Sound the trumpet, beat the drum*, contains the celebrated duet for two altos—originally sung by Mr. Abell and Mr. Turner—' Let Caesar and Urania live ', which ' continued so long in favour that succeeding composers of odes for royal birthdays were accustomed to introduce it into their own productions until after the middle of the eighteenth century '.[1] It must have been the pseudo-classic patriotism that appealed to the succeeding composers, for the music is not marvellous, in spite of a certain nobility that is never quite lacking from Purcell's music for majesty. It is the glorious finale that makes this ode noteworthy. The words as usual are poor stuff, but, as in *Dido and Aeneas*, Purcell was little hampered by such a jingle :

> To Urania and Caesar delights without measure,
> With Empire no trouble and safety with pleasure ;
> Since the joys we possess to their goodness we owe
> 'Tis but just out best wishes like that should o'erflow.

Instead of putting this jig-trot quatrain behind him with a quick jig-tune, he boldly takes each line separately and welds the whole together with a sure instinct for contrast and development that was only tentatively realized by the early symphony composers of later years.[2]

---

[1] Grove's *Dictionary*.

[2] The bare form on which this finale is built is made up as follows :
> Lines 1 and 2 Trio (repeated).
> 3 and 4 Alto solo.
> 1 and 2 Trio.
> 3 and 4 Tenor solo.
> 4   Sestet.
> 1 and 2 Chorus in seven parts (repeated).
> 3   Alto solo.
> 4   Chorus.
> Ritornello.
> 4   Chorus.

The climax comes at the first entry of the sopranos in the seven-part chorus, and the rest is practically a coda.

This ode also shows a great advance in Purcell's use of the string orchestra. Hitherto, except for an isolated solo or chorus, the orchestra was practically confined to instrumental interludes, overtures, and ritornellos, but here the choruses are fully accompanied—without the common doubling of the voice-parts—and even the recitatives are supported by the strings. Purcell was seldom slack enough to be content with bald accompaniments—his basses alone are brilliant—and once emboldened to use the orchestra with the voices he was not even content with different string parts, but made the accompaniment no less important than the voices. His skill at translating words into music has constantly been quoted, but he seldom showed such genius of perception as in the setting of the line ' His fame, like incense, mounts the skies '. The average composer—and indeed Purcell himself almost invariably —would accompany these words with ascending passages in imitation of the rising clouds of incense. But here exactly the opposite is written. The bass soloist sings an ascending passage to a top E, which he holds while the strings slowly slide downwards. The inevitable result is that the voice, softly sounding in its high register, seems by contrast with the sinking accompaniment to be mounting ever higher and higher till the last thin thread of incense melts into the sky.

Perhaps even bolder than the brilliant form of the finale and the daring use of the strings is the interpolation in this ode of a chaconne on a ground [1]—128 bars long. Instrumental ritornellos occur in the choral works as a matter of course, and independent interludes are by no means rare, but this long secession, as it were, from the matter in hand is very remarkable. Is it possible that the royal birthday guests liked to break the long stretch of musical congratulation with a dance, or was this chaconne inserted by Purcell in the vain hope that if a back-

[1] Afterwards used in *King Arthur*.

ground were provided at this point for conversation the rest of the music might be listened to in almost complete silence ? It is perhaps conceivable that these Welcome Songs bore a far closer resemblance to the ballets of the French Court and the Elizabethan Masques than is at first sight apparent, and that the performers in these congratulatory odes not only included singers and instrumentalists but at times dancers and even actors as well.[1]

It is such a constant temptation to describe a Purcell work as the finest he ever wrote, and fully a third of his compositions so surely deserve a place among the best that superlatives lose their force. But *Dido and Aeneas, The Fairy Queen,* and the great *Te Deum*—not to mention many smaller works like the *Elegy on the death of Queen Mary*—are unquestionably entitled to an equal consideration with the great music of later years. The only ode which can be entirely classed with these is known as *The Yorkshire Feast Song.* In 1687 Tillotson, Archbishop of Canterbury, preached the ' Sermon before the Feast ' at the church of St. Mary-le-Bow for the first recorded meeting of the Society of Yorkshiremen in London. From this year the Society met annually, and on 27 March 1690 at the Feast in Merchant Taylors' Hall ' a very splendid entertainment of all sorts of vocal and instrumental musick ' was given at the cost of £100.[2] This concert included an ode by D'Urfey—in his own opinion one of the finest compositions he ever made—set to music by Purcell.

This work, which celebrated the happy results of the great rebellion of 1688, is more consistently excellent than any other of Purcell's Welcome Songs or Odes. Many parts of it were printed in *Orpheus Britannicus,* it was published by Goodison in 1788, and comprises the first volume issued by the Purcell

[1] Cf. Clarke's memorial cantata, *supra,* p. 26.
[2] Advertisement in *London Gazette,* 24 Mar. 1690, and D'Urfey.

Society. Two tenor solos in *The Yorkshire Feast Song* are amazingly fine. The first—' The bashful Thames '—is a lovely example of Purcell's flute-accompanied songs : the second—' So when the glittering queen of night '—with its brilliant suggestion of a calm, moonlit sky gives yet another indication that Purcell was never so successful as when he built his melodies on a ground or some such formal basis (see p. 106). The most popular part of the ode was the manly duet for tenor and bass ' And in each track of glory ' and ' the succeeding choral burst of joy, but the alto's drum-song Sound, trumpet, sound', with its clear-cut tune, and the fine choruses—especially the fanfare finale and ' Let music join in a chorus divine ', which proves that even a ' gabble ' can be effective—are no less remarkable. The whole magnificent work shows Purcell to have had a far more sure grasp of form and style than any of his forerunners, contemporaries, or delicately scented successors.

In 1689 Purcell had begun his series of birthday odes for Queen Mary. With one exception the music to these command works is unimpressive—apart from an occasional solo or chorus —in comparison with the excellence of much of his other music. Yet considered separately the clear freshness of melody, the vigour of the choruses or overtures, and the masterly musicianship of the recitatives with the scrupulous setting and exact accentuation of the words make this series remarkable. It is as difficult to criticize Purcell's music as Bach's. Certain works may be inferior to the general bulk of the composer's music and so deserve some slight deprecation, but with a few exceptions even these must necessarily take a high place by the side of contemporary efforts. The lovely alto solo and trio from *Now the glorious Day* (1689), and the grand noble ending and the antiphonal solo and chorus in *Welcome, glorious morn* (1691) are merely exceptional beauties when compared with *The Yorkshire Feast Song* or *Ye tuneful Muses* : yet considered

TENOR SOLO.

So when the glitt'- ring Queen of

Strings.

Night with black E - clipse . . is

sha - dow'd, is sha - dow'd . . o'er.

alone even the settings of Sedley's *Love's Goddess sure* (1692) and of Tate's *Celebrate this Festival* (1693)—which indeed is well represented in *Orpheus Britannicus* and is held by some to be the finest of the Odes—deserve more than a passing word. The one exception to the comparative inferiority of these birthday odes is the admirable setting of D'Urfey's *Arise, my Muse* (1690).

Purcell's technical skill is no less apparent in this series of odes than in any other branch of his music, but his humorous ingenuity was perhaps never so well employed as in *Love's Goddess sure*. It is said that Purcell was once asked by Queen Mary to accompany the singer Arabella Hunt in the old folk-song 'Cold and Raw'. Annoyed that his own compositions should be given second place to a common ballad he determined that her Majesty should hear her favourite tune when she least expected it. He accordingly used it as the bass to the song 'May her blest example chase'. If this tale is true Purcell must have triumphed: for 'the nobility and gentry, with the lord mayor and aldermen', who were present to hear this new ode,[1] would have recognized the air with much amusement. Yet this same ode, for all its technical brilliance, has as many dull as pleasing passages.

In 1689 and 1692 Purcell added two more works to the list of his odes on music. The earlier of the two, *Celestial Music*, performed on 5 Aug. 1689 'at Mr. Maidwell's, a school-master's', is not great: indeed only the delightful alto solo 'Her charming strains' with two flutes *obbligati* need be mentioned. But the St. Cecilia Ode of 1692 *Hail, bright Cecilia*, to words by Brady, is, like *King Arthur*, a fine but uneven composition. The overture—for trumpets, hautboys, flutes, strings, and drums—is exceptional as being in five movements. It opens with a typical martial strain, followed by the

[1] Luttrell.

usual fugal Canzona.[1]   The lovely third movement is a slow
antiphon for strings and hautboys, and the overture ends with
a vigorous trumpet and drum section that is repeated after
a short coda in the minor.   The first vocal movement, after an
enunciation by a bass voice and chorus, is a fine fugal chorus,
' Fill every heart with love of thee ', broken twice by a beautiful
dual coloratura passage.   The lovely duet on a ground for alto
and bass ' Hark, each tree its silence breaks ' with the brilliant
double roulades is accompanied by two flutes and, at the
mention of the ' sprightly violin ', by that instrument.   The
florid alto solo ' 'Tis Nature's voice ' is traditionally said to have
been sung by Purcell himself, but, apart from the virtuosity
displayed by the singer, there is little interest in this over-
elaborated recitative.

This is followed by the famous chorus ' Soul of the World '.
This glorious hymn in praise of music, one of the few scraps of
Purcell that have never been forgotten, has the same grand
breadth and strong purity of style that Parry's *Blest Pair of
Sirens* shows.   It is perfect.   There is neither over-accentuation
nor lack of effect : it is full of contrast, but is exquisitely
balanced in harmony, design, and mood.   This short chorus
must without question be counted among the most sublime
works in existence.

The lovely soprano solo and chorus ' Thou tun'st this world '
is followed by three solos, a duet and trio in praise of the
different instruments of music.   The organ, ' brisk without
lightness, without dulness grave,' is given first place, but
nevertheless only inspires a dull trio.   The fine bass solo
' Wondrous machine ' praises the accompanying hautboys, and
' The airy violin ' for alto solo is almost flippant with its
clumsy sprightliness.   The ' amorous flute and soft guitar ' are

---

[1] This Canzona was transposed down a tone for the overture to *Celebrate
this Festival* in the following year.

MRS. ARABELLA HUNT *Died December* 26. 1705.

*Were there on Earth another Voice like thine, The late afflicted World some hope might have,
Another Hand so Blest with skill Divine, And Harmony recall thee from the Grave.*

V. From a print in the British Museum

immortalized in a most beautiful duet for alto and tenor, and finally ' The fife and all the harmony of war ' are given their turn in a typical alarm-song with trumpet *obbligato*. A duet for two basses brings back the general praise of music and, with a fugal interpolation—the subject of which is the same as the opening of the hymn ' All creatures of our God and King '—the original chorus to St. Cecilia brings the fine work to a grand close.

The only other two odes of any size are the unimpressive centenary work *Great Parent, Hail*, which Purcell wrote with Tate for the celebrations at Trinity College, Dublin, and the birthday ode *Who can from joy refrain* for the young Duke of Gloucester. The ' curiously poor and perfunctory work '[1] which celebrated the hundredth birthday of Trinity College, Dublin, was first performed in the College Chapel on 9 Jan. 1694.[2] It praises the memory of Queen Elizabeth and the ' Succeeding Princes ',

> But chiefly we commend to Fame
> Maria and great William's Name.

Neither Purcell nor Tate rose to any heights in this work,[3] and the birthday ode of the following year, though by no means so tedious, is not appreciably greater. The six-year-old Duke of Gloucester for whom this ode was performed on 24 July 1695 was the son of Princess Anne, who was a pupil of Purcell [4] and whose marriage to Prince George of Denmark was also celebrated by him. This pathetic little child died

---

[1] A note by Professor Mahaffy quoted in Stubbs's *History of the University of Dublin*.

[2] Stubbs.

[3] There is a theory that Purcell, like Tate, was commissioned to write this ode as being an Irishman. By analogy he should also be a Yorkshireman, as having written *The Yorkshire Feast Song*.

[4] Dedication to *Choice Collection of Lessons for the Harpsichord*, 1696.

five years later. He was weakly from a baby and at the time of these celebrations could scarcely walk without help.[1] But by a queer irony of fortune his ruling passion was a love of soldiers and fighting, and this craving, which found an outlet in the organization of small Kensington boys, is duly recognized in the ode. The finest part of the work is the magnificent final chaconne—a movement of 240 bars with an orchestra of strings, trumpets, hautboys, and bassoon, a duet, a quintet, and chorus; but it is unlikely that this last ode of Purcell will be remembered but for the cruel pathos of the small deformed creature who was so vainly apostrophized in such full terms.

5

Music for the Amateurs

PURCELL left no branch of music untouched. His operas and *Ayres for the Theatre* tickled the senses of the dramatic audiences, his anthems and services impressed the church congregations, his Welcome Songs were graciously accepted by the Court, and his St. Cecilia Odes welcomed by the musicians. He also provided instrumental music for performers on the harpsichord, strings, and organ, chamber cantatas for society enthusiasts, songs of every nature, and rounds and catches for the innumerable drinkers of London.

Some fifty catches from his pen were printed in *Catch that catch can*, *The Pleasant Musical Companion*, and many other similar collections. With the exception of seven, which are for four voices, all are for three singers. The words are by such men as Suckling, Tom Brown, Otway, and D'Urfey, but some of the verses are so needlessly coarse that the editors of the Purcell Society Edition can scarcely be blamed for an occasional

[1] *Memoirs of . . . Duke of Gloucester . . .*, John Lewis.

bowdlerization, in spite of the fact that this is the first authoritative edition of Purcell's works and as such might be expected to contain everything, good and bad. Restoration Drama is constantly said to be filthy : compared with a minority of the popular catches of the day the drama is crystal clear. A good half of the verses set by Purcell are in praise of Bacchus :

> Then stand all about, with your glasses full crown'd,
>   Till ev'rything else to our posture do grow ;
> Till over our cups and our heads,and the whole house go round
>   And the cellar become where the chamber is now.

Women are immortalized—or defamed—some nine times and the rest record some notable event or famous person.

The topical catches are interesting as showing the popular taste of the day. The Royal Family receive their due homage, the Duke of York is welcomed home, and the continual see-saw of popular favour for and against James and the Catholic Party is reflected in the words. *A Catch made in the time of Parliament*, 1676, when the Protestant Danby was in power, alludes to the fear of a Popish Plot started by the Jesuits, yet a later verse damns

> '. . . all the Whigs
> And let them be hang'd for politic prigs ;
> Both Presbyter Jack,[1] and all the whole crew,
> That lately design'd Forty-one to renew '.

As yet the time was not ripe for a repetition of the 1641 rebellion of Protestants : the leading Whigs were executed or banished, and in 1685 James II was crowned. But the later turn of the tide that preceded the flight of the Catholic king was also recorded in a catch in praise of the seven bishops

> '. . . who supported our cause,
> As stout as our martyrs, and as just as our laws '.

The refusal of the bishops to tolerate the Catholics at once

---

[1] Lauderdale.

resulted in the invitation to William of Orange and 'Great Nassau' is accordingly awarded homage. The health of the soldiers 'intrench'd on the Shannon' is celebrated, and there are two allusions to the surrender of Limerick, the last stronghold of James II in Ireland, to William III. There is much tilting at the French, King Louis, Vauban, the engineer who fortified Charleroi, the siege of which is mentioned, and Madame de Maintenon, and there is one allusion to the long struggle between the Turks and the German allies. People of less national importance celebrated in these catches are the two publishers John Playford and John Carr with his ' maggotman Sam', whose names occur in *A Catch by way of Epistle* that was prefixed to the first book of *Comes Amoris* (1687), and ' Mr. Anthony Hall, who keeps the Mermaid Tavern in *Oxford*, and plays his part very well on the Violin ', whose name is paraphrased into a rebus and then set to music. There is, besides, this admirable condensation of the impressions of the famous Bartholomew Fair :

Here 's that will challenge all the Fair ;
Come buy my nuts and damsons, my Burgamy pears :
Here 's the whore of Babylon, the Devil, and the Pope ;
The girl is just a-going on the rope.

Here 's Dives and Lazarus and the world's creation ;
Here 's the Dutch woman, the like 's not in the nation ;
Here is the booth where the tall Dutch maid is ;
Here are bears that dance like any ladies.

' To-to-to-to-tot ', goes the little penny trumpet ;
Here 's your Jacob Hall [1] that can jump it, jump it ;
Sound, trumpet, sound ; a silver spoon and fork ;
Come, here 's your dainty pig and pork.

For the polite singers of the day Purcell wrote a number of ' single songs '—that is, songs that do not depend on any dramatic or sacred context—and chamber cantatas. The

---

[1] Famous as one of Lady Castlemain's lovers. *Vide* Pepys and Grammont.

cantata, which seems tiresome enough to us with its long
figures, points of imitation, and uninspiring sentiment, was in
the seventeenth century the most popular form of chamber
music. Corelli, Vivaldi, and Geminiani, the first great violinists,
were younger contemporaries of Purcell and as yet had no
opportunity to make the violin a popular instrument. The
older bowed instruments, though charming, did not give much
scope for brilliant performers, and the harpsichord, the tone of
which tended to be monotonous except in the hands of a real
genius, was little better. The voice then was the only instrument that could be used to perform show pieces, and accordingly the chamber cantata enjoyed a century's popularity
before it was ousted by the violin sonata and the string quartet.

Purcell's cantatas were written for one or two voices. Almost
all the duets are for soprano and bass, and usually deal with
a more or less pastoral setting of love. Some actually take the
form of a pastoral dialogue between Strephon and Dorinda or
Alexis and Sylvia ; in others—such as the lovely *Serenading Song*
with two flutes—there is no characterization between the
different voices, while two concern the more dramatic con-
versations of Love and Despair or Charon and Orpheus. Most
of the cantatas, both for solo voice and duet, are of great length.
Indeed in the majority the length tends to blur the charm of
the music. The two pastoral duets *How sweet is the air* and
How pleasant is this flow'ry plain are charming, and the most
intricately accompanied *See where she sits* is by no means
hampered by its great length. *What can we poor females do*
is an amusing trifle—especially as both singers are male—and
Lost is my quiet is lovely. But by far the finest of all the duets,
if not the finest piece of music ever written by Purcell, is the
superb *Elegy for Queen Mary*.

This work for two sopranos is in four short movements. The
first—'O Dive custos Auriacae Domus'—is unavoidably

reminiscent of the breadth and grasp of Purcell's successor, Bach.

Nothing can be gained by a comparison between the two. Both were masters of their art in their own particular way. Purcell was essentially a composer of dramatic and objective music, Bach's music was subjective and aimed at the sublime, whether of religion or art. Purcell wrote programme music and treated all human passions as brilliantly as he turned a calm sea into music. Heaven to him was but one of the myriad facets of mortal and immortal truths that could be reflected by his art. With Bach the ideal came first : the voices for which he wrote—though in practice the faulty human voices of the choir—were on paper the great original voices of which all others are copies : the translation of passions and actions into music, which was part of the essence of Purcell's scheme, was but incidental to Bach. Purcell was writing in a medium that was new, for instruments that were new and in a style that was new, but Bach, who was ten years old at Purcell's death,[1] dismissed the new melodic style of writing and—through the chance of the time of his birth— was able to bring the polyphonic style to perfection : the new stringed instruments were fairly accepted by the beginning of the eighteenth century, and opera, with its attendant realistic music, was well established if Bach had chosen to adopt it.

[1] Wagner also was ten years old when Beethoven died.

No comparison can be made between the two composers, they can only be contrasted. The wonder is that Purcell, writing from such an opposite point of view to Bach's, could by different means achieve as powerful an effect in the very style in which the later composer was supreme.

The second movement ' Seu te fluentem pronus ad Isida ', a peaceful, flowing movement in triple time in which the voices sing together, is followed by a quasi-recitative ' Maria musis flebilis occidit '. It is in the last movement ' O flete Mariam Camoenae ' that the mood—if not the music—is strongly reminiscent of Bach's amazing ' Crucifixus ' from the *B minor Mass*,

and the last marvellous bars are as poignant as any great requiem and yet their dramatic power is full of sincerity without the least touch of artificiality (see musical example on p. 118).

Four of the solo cantatas are elegies. One was written *on the Death of his worthy friend Mr. Matthew Locke* : John Playford, the publisher, is commemorated in *A pastoral*

elegy under the name of Theron: the bachelor of music
Thomas Farmer is likewise mourned as Thirsis, and Queen
Mary is again lamented. By far the finest is the elegy on
Playford, and the longest, most extraordinary and most tedious
memorial work—it can hardly be called an elegy—is the
amazing cantata called *Sighs for our late Sovereign King Charles
the Second*.

A Pastoral Coronation Song for 1685 and an ode to the
Queen in 1690 are the two serious historical compositions for
a solo voice, and a very ribald song records an imaginary conversation between *A grasshopper and a fly* as to the parentage
of the latter. The fly, whose other names were 'Jemmy
Scott', Duke of Monmouth, claims royal Phoebus for his
father, but the grasshopper King James, though he admits that
possibility, is equally vehement that the fly was not so purely
descended on the other side. The enthusiasts who claim Irish
descent for Purcell will be glad to find a song with a distinctly

Irish cadence, but Scottish ancestry is equally apparent in more than one song—notably in the jolly *Sawney is a bonny lad*, which was sung with the St. Cecilia Ode for 1692 at the concert that was held on 25 Jan. 1694 in York Buildings in honour of Prince Lewis of Baden. Purcell was especially fond of a poem with the familiar first line *If music be the food of love*, for he has left three different settings. His other songs vary from the ' brigadiers and cavalry ' of the fine *Anacreon's Defeat* and the madness of *Bess of Bedlam*—which is little more than a brilliant study in characterization, to the charm of *An Ode to Cynthia walking on Richmond Hill* and *Lucinda is bewitching fair*, which was sung by the famous Mr. Bowen at the opening of the Old Play-House. Finally there is a second ' last Song that Mr. Henry Purcell sett before he dy'd ',[1] *Lovely Albina's come ashore*, dealing no doubt with the reconciliation of Princess Anne (lovely !) to the ' Belgick lion ', William III.

A number of the ' single songs ' together with extracts from the more famous of the operas and odes were collected after Purcell's death by his widow and published under the title of *Orpheus Britannicus*. Mrs. Purcell dedicated the volume to ' the Honourable The Lady Howard '.[2]

' Your Ladyship's extraordinary Skill in Music beyond most of either Sex, and Your great Goodness to that dear Person, whom You have sometimes been pleased to honour with the Title of Your Master, makes it hard for me to judge whither *(sic)* he contributed more to the vast Improvements You have made in that Science, or Your Ladyship to the Reputation he gained in the Profession of it : For I have often heard him say, That as several of his best Compositions were originally design'd for Your Ladyship's Entertainment, so the Pains he bestowed in fitting them for Your Ear, were abundantly rewarded by the Satisfaction he has received from Your Approbation, and admirable performance of

[1] See p. 92.

[2] Probably ' the Lady Howard ' in question was Dryden's wife.

ORPHEUS BRITANNICUS.

A

COLLECTION

OF ALL

The Choicest SONGS

FOR

One, Two, and Three Voices,

COMPOS'D

By Mr. Henry Purcell.

TOGETHER,

With such Symphonies for *Violins* or *Flutes*,

As were by Him design'd for any of them :

AND

A *THROUGH-BASS* to each Song;

Figur'd for the *Organ*, *Harpsichord*, or *Theorbo-Lute*.

All which are placed in their several Keys according to the
Order of the *Gamut*.

LONDON,

Printed by *J. Heptinstall*, for *Henry Playford*, in the *Temple-Change*,
in *Fleet-street*, MDCXCVIII.

VI. Title-page of the 1698 ed. of Purcell's *Orpheus Britannicus*

them, which has best recommended both them and their
Author to all that have had the Happiness of hearing them
from Your Ladyship.

Another great Advantage to which my Husband has often
imputed the Success of his Labors . . . has been the great
Justness both of Thought and Numbers which he found in
the Poetry of our most refin'd Writers, and among them,
of that Honourable Gentleman, who has the dearest and
most deserved Relation to Your Self, and whose Excellent
Compositions were the Subject of his last and best Performance in Music.'

That Purcell ' often imputed the Success of his Labors ' to
the excellence of the poetry he set is surprising in view of the
feeble verses with which he was so often provided, but, as
the publisher of the second edition of *Orpheus Britannicus*
wrote,

' *The Author's extraordinary Tallent in all sorts of* Music,
is sufficiently known ; but he was particularly admir'd for his
Vocal, *having a peculiar Genius to express the Energy of*
English Words, *whereby he mov'd the Passions as well as
caus'd Admiration in all his Auditors.*'

This special skill is again recorded in one of the many com-
memorative poems with which the various editions of this
work are full :

Each Syllable first weigh'd, or short, or long,
That it might too be Sense, as well as Song.

Mrs. Purcell also published a *Choice Collection of Lessons for
the Harpsichord* after her husband's death, and dedicated this
volume to another of his pupils, Princess Anne of Denmark.
This book contains an explanation of the notes of the keyboard
of the instrument, the meaning of the printed notes, rests,
and musical terms, the different indications of tempo, a translation into ordinary notation of the numerous graces with which
the music was embellished and a careful illustration of the best

fingering of scales for the harpsichord. These instructions are
exceedingly valuable in enabling musicians of to-day to realize
more nearly the true effect of seventeenth-century keyboard
music in England, but perhaps the most remarkable is the
illustration of the fingering :

(N.B. in R.H. 1 = thumb, 5 = little finger, &c.
L.H. 1 = little finger, 5 = thumb, &c.)

It seems incredible that rapid passages can have been played
on this principle, but the description is explicit enough.

It is interesting to see by the keys in which Purcell wrote
his harpsichord pieces which were those more frequently used.
G major, C major, and D minor are the more usual, and of
the seven others that he employs E minor, F major, and
A major only occur once each. His sense of key was strong,
but the principle of key-relationship was as yet but dimly
realized. He would at times venture some little way from the

key of the piece inside the piece itself, but he rarely dared to take the risk of staying far from the master-key for any length of time. His eight Suites for the Harpsichord are all rigidly built in their respective keys, even the individual movements being religiously confined to the same keys.

Five of these Suites consist of four movements and are all built on the same model: Prelude, Almand, Corant, and a dance—either a Minuet or Saraband. The Preludes are usually fugal and in one section: their length varies from nine to thirty-seven bars. The other movements are in two sections: the Almands of a similarly varied length, the Corants all over twenty bars long, and the last movements—more melodic than the others—vary between sixteen and twenty bars. Of the other three Suites, two consist of a Prelude, an Almand, and a Corant or Hornpipe, while one is made up of an Almand, a Corant, and a Hornpipe. It should be noted that Purcell's Hornpipes—perhaps the most successful of his dances—are in triple time, the well-known ' sailors' hornpipe ' rhythm not being known till the middle of the eighteenth century.

Besides these Suites there exist some twenty-nine original harpsichord pieces by Purcell.[1] There are five Airs, two Almands, a Borry, a Corant, two Grounds, a Hornpipe, two Lessons,[2] a March, five Minuets, a Prelude, a Rigaddon, a Toccata, two Trumpet Tunes—one a famous piece known as the *Cebell*, a Song Tune, a Scotch Tune, ' A New Irish Tune '—the notorious *Lilliburlero*, a piece called ' Sefauchi's Farewell ', and ' The Queen's Dolour, A Farewell '. The delicacy and charm of these pieces are so great that no differen-

[1] Eight pieces that are printed as harpsichord pieces are arrangements from his other works, three are not by Purcell, and three are probably organ works.

[2] These have no titles. Most of these separate pieces were published in Playford's *Musick's Handmaid*, 1689.

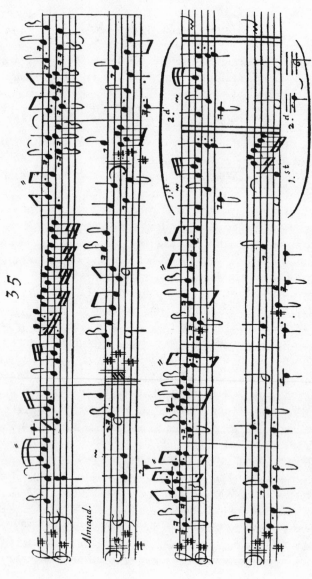

VII. From *A Choice Collection of Lessons for the Harpischord or Spinnet*. Printed on Copper Plates for Mrs. Frances Purcell . . . London, 1696.

tiation can be made, except to say that perhaps three are not quite as pleasant as the rest. The Minuet given here is

&c.

typical of these delightful miniatures : Purcell in such moods as this is the musical parallel of Horace, for the natural ease of his airs is as fresh as Mozart's, his means are even simpler and his musicianship at least as great.

Lilliburlero became historically famous, and the *Cebell*—a fine piece of noble music—was musically famous. ' Sefauchi's Farewell ' is perhaps chiefly worth remembering as a musical compliment to the famous male soprano, Giovanni Francesco Grossi, who was known as ' Siface ', through his great success in that role. He stayed in England from 18 January–16 June in 1687, and sang in the Chapel to James II.[1] By far the finest harpsichord work is the magnificent Toccata. This is a long piece—105 bars—in five continuous movements. The first is a bravura movement in which the two hands answer each other in rippling passages which gather speed and power till together they rush downwards to a fine close. The second movement is a bold fugue built on a grand arpeggiac theme (see p. 126) : again comes the gathering rush, which this time quietens to a soft rocking which flows straight into a rhythmic swaying. This, too, gathers speed and power, but is stopped by a short section of dramatic instrumental recitative. Without a

[1] E. J. Dent, *Scarlatti*.

break the last movement begins with a care-free play of glancing light and shade : the ripples grow until there is swirl upon swirl of notes—reminiscent of the recitative—and the Toccata

comes to a grand finish to give the final proof—if proof is needed—that Purcell was indeed a master of music with more breadth and power than all his contemporaries.

The organ, as we know it, was then in its infancy, though organs of sorts had been in existence for years. In Purcell's time there were four types. The first had only a single manual and the shifting movement required to take off the stops in use naturally did not make for frequent or rapid variety of tone. The other single manual organ was provided with stops which drew in halves and accordingly affected either the treble or the bass as a whole. The double organ, however, with two manuals, afforded the possibility of a considerable amount of rapid changes, while the occasional addition of a third manual called the ' eccho ' organ made a number of dramatic effects possible, and was no doubt responsible for Purcell's many experiments with the echo ending of which he was so fond.

Luckily among the few organ pieces of Purcell that are known there are examples for each of these types of organ. The single manual with the shifting action is represented by a Voluntary in D minor in which the effects are made by semiquaver and demisemiquaver runs under and above a pedal point. The *Voluntary of the* 100*th Psalm*—a fine, if somewhat austere work—is most interesting as showing the technique required for the second type of organ—the single manual with stops. The piece starts with the normal Diapason tone and the half-stop (15th bass) for the bass entry, while the Cornet is added—allowing a half-bar's rest for the necessary manipulation—for the Treble entry of the chorale.

It is interesting to notice how cleverly Purcell has avoided overlapping into the lowest Cornet note (C natural) in the short interludes between the entries of the tune. There is a fine *Voluntary for the Double Organ* which is differentiated from the others by the crossing of the hands—an obvious impossibility on a single manual, and a short *Voluntary in C major* [1] shows the treatment for the ' eccho organ '.[2]

In 1683, Purcell, as ' *Composer in Ordinary to his most Sacred Majesty, and* Organist of his *CHAPPELL ROYALL* ', pub-

---

[1] Said to be Purcell's.

[2] Purcell's own organ, ' Single Spinnett ' and ' double Spiñet ', were left to his son by his widow.

lished a set of ' Sonnata's of III Parts '. This publication was headed by a letter To the Reader :

'Ingenuous Reader,|*Instead of an elaborate harangue on the beauty and the charms of Musick (which after all the learned Encomions that words can contrive commends it self best by the performances of a skilful hand, and an angelical voice :) I shall say but a very few things by way of Preface, concerning the following Book, and its Author : for its Author, he has faithfully endea vour'd a just imitation of the most fam'd Italian Masters ; principally, to bring the seriousness and gravity of that sort of Musick into vogue, and reputation among our Country-men, whose humor, 'tis time now, should begin to loath the levity, and balladry of our neighbours : The attempt he confesses to be bold, and daring, there being Pens and Artists of more eminent abilities, much better qualify'd for the imployment than his, or himself, which he well hopes these his weak endeavours, will in due time provoke, and enflame to a more acurate undertaking. He is not asham'd to own his unskilfulness in the Italian Language ; but that's the unhappiness of his Education, which cannot justly be accounted his fault, however he thinks he may warrantably affirm, that he is not mistaken in the power of the Italian Notes, or elegancy of their Compositions, which he would recommend to the English Artists. There has been neither care, nor industry wanting, as well in contriving, as revising the whole Work ; which had been abroad in the world much sooner, but that he has now thought fit to cause the whole Thorough Bass to be Engraven, which was a thing quite besides his first Resolutions. It remains only that the English Practitioner be enform'd, that he will find a few terms of Art perhaps unusual to him, the chief of which are these following :* Adagio *and* Grave, *which import nothing but a very slow movement :* Presto Largo, Poco Largo, *or* Largo *by it self, a middle movement :* Allegro, *and* Vivace, *a very brisk, swift, or fast movement :* Piano, *soft. The Author has no more to add, but his hearty wishes, that his Book may fall into no other hands but theirs who carry Musical Souls about them ; for he is willing to flatter himself into a belief, that with such his labours will seem neither unpleasant, nor unprofitable.* Vale.'

It is a puzzle to know what Italian models Purcell took[1]— if any. Very few Italian sets of sonatas were published before 1683, the usual string music being ' Balletti ' in an embryonic Suite form which were not meant to be played in succession. The sonatas that show the most kinship to Purcell's are those of Vitali, which were published in 1677, but the likeness is rather general than particular. The form of Purcell's sonatas is as follows : A slowish or maestoso movement—with no verbal indication of speed—which resembles the martellato movement of pointed notes belonging to the French overture. A fugal movement named *Canzona*, which appears anywhere but first, and is preceded or followed by a slow movement, usually a Largo in triple time. A short Grave section is often used to introduce the *Canzona* or to end the whole sonata. Curious time-signatures are used which probably indicate the pace and rhythmic division,[2] and which have no Italian counterpart.[3]

It is curious that the keys of these sonatas occur in this sequence :

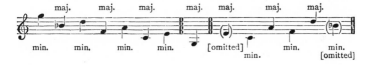

The circle could not be fully completed, as E major and B flat minor were at the time practically impossible to work in. This may seem unnecessarily complicated, but Purcell so con-

---

[1] Purcell, in his additions to Playford's *Introduction to the Skill of Musick*, quotes a fugue from the works of ' the famous ' Lelio Corista, of whom nothing is known beyond his manuscript sonatas at the British Museum, Christ Church, and the Bodleian.

[2] Cf. Dolmetsch, *Interpretation of Music in the Sixteenth and Seventeenth Centuries*.

[3] W. Barclay Squire, *Musical Times*, Apr. 1917.

stantly loved to tie his hands with some mathematical or musical
riddle such as a ground bass or well-known tune hidden under
counterpoint, not to mention canons two in one on a ground,
that some such device as this must have appealed to him, though
its musical—or even intellectual—value is negligible. Indeed
the sixth Sonata contains a ' Canon by twofold augmentation
in the 5th and 8th above ',

and Richard Clarke (1780–1856) went to the effort of finding a
hidden jig-saw of *God Save the King* in this work :[1] this may

[1] In MS. score R.C.M.

have been far-fetched, but if it does not really exist it certainly ought, and Purcell would have been the first to acclaim it.

There is no need to say more of Purcell's string music, but that it is all admirable. It is fresh, dramatic, sincere, and masterly. Each sonata—of three parts or of four [1]—contains some new surprising beauty. The daring brilliance of the minor ending to the sonata of three parts in D major,

---

[1] These Sonatas in four parts (published in 1696) only differ from those of three parts in that the *continuo* part of the former is not always identical with the string bass.

the inverted pedal at the end of the fourth Sonata in four parts,

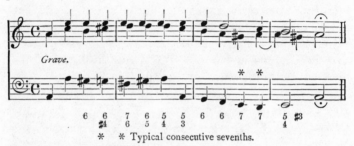

Grave.

6   6   7   6   5   5   6   6   7   7   5   ♯3
     ♯4   6   5   4   3   4

*   * Typical consecutive sevenths.

and the real pedal at the end of the fifth,

6   6   6   5   ♯   ♯3   6   5   6   ♮6   7
     4   4   ♯3   ♯3   4   5

♮7   ♮6   ♭9   ♮9   ♯7   8   ♭9   ♮9   5   6   4   5
     ♮   ♮6   ♯3   ♯   4   ♯   ♮   3   3

are strokes of genius.

The string technique displayed in the later works is interesting. The early works might almost have been written for viols as far as the leaps are concerned, but in the later sonatas are found true violin passages, as this example from the tenth sonatas in four parts :

The *Fantazias* in three, four,[1] and five parts (1680), the two *In Nomines* in six and seven parts, and the lovely *Pavan* and *Chacony* in four parts are at last very slowly beginning to be known. The musical world is sadly ignorant at the present time of seventeenth-century instrumental music ; it would be excellent if the *Fantazias* could be the first examples to be studied—rather than the lovely but unexceptional *Golden Sonata*.

It seems strange that there is no other kind of music by Purcell to be skimmed through here. Yet every branch of music has been touched except works for solo instruments—apart from the harpsichord,—symphonic works for an orchestra and chamber works for other instruments than strings. These are indeed the only realms of music into which Purcell did not venture—though he came to their borders in his dramatic music. It is tiresome to insist on his excellence in every branch of music, and it would be foolish to pretend—as Bach lovers pretend—that every note he wrote was masterly. Both Purcell and Bach, like their lesser followers, have their weak moments, but, as with Bach, Purcell's weak moments were exceedingly few, and in almost every example these defects can be laid to the door of the librettist or the occasion.

As I have repeatedly said before, Purcell's genius was essentially dramatic—or, if some musicians dislike a taste of the

[1] The *Fantazias* of four parts are dated as follows : 10th, 11th, 14th, 19th, 22nd, 23rd, 30th June, 18th, 31st Aug. 1680, and 24th Feb. 1682-3.

VIII. *Fantasia* for Four Strings in the autograph of Henry Purcell,
Add. MS. 30930.

theatre, I will call it human. Purcell could feel with his singers and actors, and could love the beauties and dread the horrors of the world more intensely than most of the city madams and fine gentlemen of Tuttle Street. Beside this intense human kindness, he was gifted with a masterly power of technique. His hand was so sure that his musicianship never obtrudes and masks his infinite sincerity. His craftsmanship was so easy to him that he could not see that it might be difficult to others. In his additions to Playford's *Skill of Musick* he left till last what has not been stressed in this book —the ground bass. Far from being hampered by this device he was almost always more successful when he employed it. His last words on this matter will equally serve as the last words to this book:

' One Thing that was forgot to be spoken of in its proper Place, I think necessary to say a little of now, which is, Composing upon a *Ground*, a very easy thing to do, and requires but little Judgment ; as 'tis generally used in *Chacones*, and often the *Ground* is four Notes gradually descending, but to maintain *Fuges* upon it would be difficult, being confin'd like a *Canon* to a *Plain Song*. There are also pretty *Dividing Grounds* (of whom the *Italians* where (*sic*) the first Inventors) to Single *Songs*, or *Songs* of Two Parts which to do neatly, requires considerable Pains, and the best way to be acquainted with 'em, is to score much, and chuse the best Authors.

As for *Fugeing*, 'tis done by the same Methods as has been before observ'd.

All that I shall further add, is to wish, That what is hear (*sic*) mention'd may be Useful as 'tis Intended, and then 'twill more than Recompence the Trouble of the Author.

Finis.'

THE PURCELL FAMILY

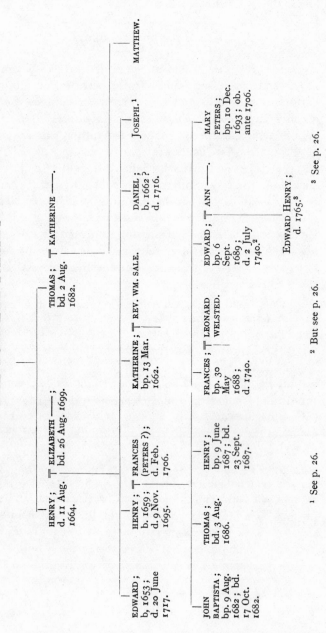

¹ See p. 26.   ² But see p. 26.   ³ See p. 26.